First World War
and Army of Occupation
War Diary
France, Belgium and Germany

1 DIVISION
1 Infantry Brigade
London Regiment
14th (County of London) Battalion (London Scottish)
4 August 1914 - 31 January 1916

WO95/1266/2

The Naval & Military Press Ltd

Published by

The Naval & Military Press Ltd

Unit 10 Ridgewood Industrial Park,

Uckfield, East Sussex,

TN22 5QE England

Tel: +44 (0) 1825 749494

www.naval-military-press.com

www.nmarchive.com

Contents

War Diary	Cambrin Bethune	17/06/1915	17/06/1915
War Diary	Bethune	18/06/1915	18/06/1915
War Diary	Bethune-Lapugnoy	19/06/1915	20/06/1915
War Diary	Lapugnoy	21/06/1915	23/06/1915
War Diary	Lapugnoy Hurionville	24/06/1915	24/06/1915
War Diary	Hurionville	25/06/1915	28/06/1915
War Diary	Hurionville-Fouquereuil	29/06/1915	29/06/1915
War Diary	Fouquereuil	30/06/1915	30/06/1915
Map			
Heading	1st Infantry Brigade 1st Division War Diary London Scottish (14th London Regiment) July 1915		
War Diary	Fouquereuil	01/07/1915	05/07/1915
War Diary	Vermelles	06/07/1915	19/07/1915
War Diary	Bethune	20/07/1915	25/07/1915
War Diary	Cambrin	26/07/1915	31/07/1915
Heading	1st Infantry Brigade 1st Division War Diary London Scottish (14th London Regiment) August 1915		
War Diary	Cambrin	01/08/1915	06/08/1915
War Diary	Bret River Camp Near Fouquieres	07/08/1915	12/08/1915
War Diary	Vermelles	13/08/1915	24/08/1915
War Diary	Verquin	25/08/1915	31/08/1915
Diagram etc			
Map			
Heading	1st Brigade War Diary Of London Scottish September 1915		
War Diary	Les Pesses	01/09/1915	21/09/1915
War Diary	Verquin	23/09/1915	24/09/1915
War Diary	Vermelles Fosse Way	25/09/1915	30/09/1915
War Diary	Noeux-Les-Mines	30/09/1915	30/09/1915
War Diary		25/09/1915	25/09/1915
Map			
Heading	1st Infantry Brigade. 1st Division London Scottish (14th London Regiment) September 1915		
War Diary	Lespesse	01/09/1915	30/09/1915
Miscellaneous	Appendices 1 1a 2 3 4 5 5a 6 7 7a (8-9 Missing) 10		
Miscellaneous	A Form Messages And Signals.	25/09/1915	25/09/1915
Miscellaneous	18th Inf/Bde	15/09/1915	15/09/1915
Miscellaneous	A Form. Messages And Signals.	25/09/1915	25/09/1915
Miscellaneous	London Scottish	25/09/1915	25/09/1915
Miscellaneous	Operation Orders By	25/09/1915	25/09/1915
Miscellaneous	A Form. Messages And Signals.	25/09/1915	25/09/1915
Diagram etc			
Miscellaneous	A Form. Messages And Signals.	25/09/1915	25/09/1915
Miscellaneous	A Form. Messages And Signals.	26/09/1915	26/09/1915
Miscellaneous	A Form. Messages And Signals.		
Map			
Heading	1st Infantry Brigade. 1st Division War Diary London Scottish (14th London Regiment) October 1915		
War Diary	Noeux-Les-Mines	01/10/1915	05/10/1915
War Diary	W Of Hulluch	05/10/1915	14/10/1915
War Diary	Lillers	15/10/1915	23/10/1915
Miscellaneous	Appendices 1 To 10 Inc.		
Miscellaneous	To O.C. London Scottish	07/10/1915	07/10/1915
Map			
Miscellaneous			
Miscellaneous	A Form. Messages And Signals.	13/10/1915	13/10/1915

Miscellaneous	A Form. Messages And Signals.		
Miscellaneous	A Form. Messages And Signals.	13/10/1915	13/10/1915
Miscellaneous			
Miscellaneous	A Form. Messages And Signals.	14/10/1915	14/10/1915
Miscellaneous	Instruction For Attack	12/10/1915	12/10/1915
Miscellaneous	Instructions For Attack	11/10/1915	11/10/1915
Heading	1st Infantry Brigade 1st Division War Diary London Scottish (14th London Regiment) November 1915		
War Diary	Lillers	01/11/1915	18/11/1915
War Diary	Mazingarbe	19/11/1915	30/11/1915
Heading	1st Infantry Brigade 1st Division War Diary London Scottish (14th London Regiment) December 1915		
War Diary		01/12/1915	03/12/1915
War Diary	Philosophe	03/12/1915	09/12/1915
War Diary	Noeux-Les-Mines	09/12/1915	24/12/1915
War Diary	Philosophe	21/12/1915	27/12/1915
War Diary	Noeux-Les-Mines	27/12/1915	31/12/1915
Miscellaneous	Appendices 1 To 4		
Miscellaneous	Operation Orders By Lt. Col. B.G. Green 6 M G T D	05/12/1915	05/12/1915
Miscellaneous			
Miscellaneous	1st Infantry Brigade	24/12/1915	24/12/1915
Heading	1st Brigade 1st Division Transferred To 56th Division 7.2.16 1/14th Battalion London Regiment (London Scottish) January 1916		
Heading	1st Div 1st Bde 1/14 London Regt Jan Vol XVI 70 56 Div 7.2.16		
War Diary	Noeux-Les-Mines	01/01/1916	01/01/1916
War Diary	At Philosophe	02/01/1916	15/01/1916
War Diary	Burbure	15/01/1916	31/01/1916

WO 95 / 1266 / 2.

1-14TH BATTALION

THE LONDON REGIMENT

(LONDON SCOTTISH)

AUG - DEC 1914

To 56 DIV
168 Bde

1st Brigade.

1st Division.

1/14th BATTALION

THE LONDON REGIMENT

(LONDON SCOTTISH)

4th AUGUST to 29th SEPTEMBER

1 9 1 4

Instructions regarding War Diaries and Intelligence Summaries are contained in F.S. Regs., Part II. and the Staff Manual respectively. Title pages will be prepared in manuscript.

WAR DIARY
or
INTELLIGENCE SUMMARY.
(Erase heading not required.)

Army Form C. 2118.

14th TDR Sherwood Regts

Hour, Date, Place	Summary of Events and Information	Remarks and references to Appendices
August 4th	The 14th (Serv) Bn Sherwood Foresters received orders to mobilise and on Aug. 17th moved into Billets at WATFORD and ST ALBANS.	
" 17th		
September 15th.	Entrained for Southampton. Embarked on S.S. WINEFREDIAN for HAVRE.	The Bn wrote letters to excellent
(Sailed 7.30 pm. 15th) S.S. WINEFREDIAN	Strength of the Bn 31 officers - 921 other ranks - Br. Maj. Ammn & Bn other ranks were left at Southampton with kit bags by order of Embarking Staff. Transport consisted of 16 vehicles (including 2 machine guns) - 59 horses.	worked among the wounded and the dressing of wounds. Then operations were carried out by Capt. MacNab. R.A.M.C. Tr.
Sept. 16. 7 a.m.	Arrived at HAVRE. After disembarking line awaited instructions all day and on reaching them G. F. & H Coys were entrained about 7 pm for LE MANS. In charge of Majors B.S. Green & J.H. Jorrance. Transport accompanying them detached were 2 waggons & say 6 Packanimals.	Sgt. Wright. Act. R.T.O. front (who has now become a temporary R.A.T.O. Commander. The regular R.A.T.O. Staff was quite unable to cope with the hundreds of wounds who were arriving daily, many of this time from the Battle of the Aisne.
	The Bn with transport less G. F & H Coys and their transport entrained about 9 pm for VILLENEUVE ST. GEORGES. (advanced Replenishing Base)	
Sept. 17th.	Arrived VILLENEUVE. 9.30 am on the 17th.	
Sept. 19th	The following moves were made. E Company under Captain J.H. Lindsay & Lt. Duncan moved to FER - EN - TARDENOIS which was also the position of G.H.Q.	Lt. G. Malcom is appointed Commandant of VILLENEUVE VILLAGE. VILLENEUVE ST FRONT
Moved of E, B, D Coys.	B Coy (Capt. J.B. Cartwright, Lt. Strathnairn Taylor) moved to OUCHY - BRESNY & D Coy (Lt. Blaikie, Lt. Frost) moved to billets at NEUILLY - ST - FRONT	

(9.20.6) W 2794 100,000 8/14 HWV   Forms/C. 2118/11.

Army Form C. 2118.

WAR DIARY
or
INTELLIGENCE SUMMARY.
(Erase heading not required.)

Instructions regarding War Diaries and Intelligence Summaries are contained in F.S. Regs., Part II. and the Staff Manual respectively. Title pages will be prepared in manuscript.

14 th Bde. Northumberland Regt

September

Hour, Date, Place	Summary of Events and Information	Remarks and references to Appendices
H. Sept. 22nd. moved ½ D Coy, ½ D Coy	½ D Coy under Lt Taylor moved to MONT - NOTRE - DAME as ½ D Coy under Lt front moved to OUCHY. BRESNY.	
Sept. 25th. Return of RE MANS de Crehunde.	G, H, J Companies returned to Head Qrs from LEMANS, but G & H Coys under Major Torrance were sent on at once to ORLEANS for duties with Indian troops arriving from MARSEILLES. Major B.C. Green & J Company (Capt Dunsmore + Lt Balmer) joined Hd. Qrs. Lt ALLSOP with a ½ Company composed of J, G, H Companies has proceeded to BRAINE with re-inforcements to the front. Lt ALLSOP was his ½ Coy were retained there for RAILHEAD duty until the completion of the movement to the north about Oct. 15th.	
Sept. 29th.	½ D Coy under Lt front rejoins.	Oct. 15th ALLSOP move broken Dunkinstone.

1st Brigade.
1st Division.

1/14th BATTALION

LONDON REGIMENT

"The London Scottish"

OCTOBER 1 9 1 4

Army Form C. 2118

3

October 1914

WAR DIARY
or
INTELLIGENCE SUMMARY.
(Erase heading not required.)

Instructions regarding War Diaries and Intelligence Summaries are contained in F.S. Regs., Part II. and the Staff Manual respectively. Title pages will be prepared in manuscript.

Hour, Date, Place	Summary of Events and Information	Remarks and references to Appendices
October 1st	Still performing duties on lines of Communication at VILLENEUVE. ST. GEORGE.	
Oct. 5th.	G & H Companies under Brig. Servaus return from Orleans.	
" 8th moved	½ B. A Company under Capt. Macdonald, Lt. Stirling, Lt. Frost, Lt. Walker recede into & move to BOULOGNE ETAPLES	
½ D Coy. ½ D Coy.	½ B Coy under Capt. Cartwright Lt. Stretting move to CREPY-EN-VALOIS	
" "	½ D Coy under Lt. Blaikie rejoin Hd Qs	
" "	E Coy move from toulhus at FER-EN-TARDENOIS to ABBEVILLE	Lt. ALLSOP to still at BRAINE
Oct. 14th.	The following moves take place. C & F Companies move to BOULOGNE under the Command of Lt. Torrance and G & F Coys transport with him as follows, 1 wagon, 1 watercart & packanimals. G Company under Capt. Monro & Lt. Farquharson move to ROUEN with transport of 1 wagon & 2 packanimals	
Oct. 14th dep. VILLENEUVE 9.46 pm en. ABBEVILLE 11 a.m.	Head Qrs of the Battalion & its transport & details above referred to, move to ABBEVILLE. Where Hqs arrive 11 a.m.	C/Mallcom assumes Command of Troops ABBEVILLE. Capt. Cartwright assumes the duties of Assistant Provost Marshall.
	A1 E Coy & 1B Coy have already arrived at ABBEVILLE but now again on two dates.	
Oct. 23.	Lt. Paterson with 1 Sergt of Homen religion 1 Stretcher & Armen proceeding to HAVRE with 170 German Prisoners	P.H. & Qs D Coys
Oct. 24.	Lt. Lindsay — Reinft with American proceed with 60 men & 6 J.N.O & 2 cent & 6 J.N.O & 2 cent of 400 German Prisoners	P.H. D Cap

ww. W301 100,000 8/14 H W V   Forms/C. 2118/11.

WAR DIARY

or

INTELLIGENCE SUMMARY.

(Erase heading not required.)

Instructions regarding War Diaries and Intelligence
Summaries are contained in F. S. Regs., Part II.
and the Staff Manual respectively. Title pages
will be prepared in manuscript.

Hour, Date, Place	Summary of Events and Information	Remarks and references to Appendices
Oct. 27th	The Bn received orders of Concentrate at ST OMER when they arrived at midnight.	
Oct. 29th	The Bn was moved my motor buses through the night to YPRES.	Lt Palmer Lt fudsay Lt Capt Browne Capt Lindsay Lt Ker-Pollard, did not accompany the Bn as it was most unfit 1st + 2nd inc handcart
Oct. 30th	The Bn marched to HOGGE East of YPRES where it came under the orders of GEN MONRO + GEN BULFIN. About 4pm it marched back to YPRES and in motor buses was taken to ST ELOI where it was placed under the orders of GEN GOUGH and GEN VAUGHAN. The Bn was billetted during 30th/31st Oct at ST ELOI	
Oct. 31st	At 6 am, the Bn moved under GEN GOUGH's orders to WYTSCHAETR. About 8.30 am it moved more through WYTSCHAETR towards MESSINES in order to make a counter attack through the Cavalry trenches. This move was carried out under heavy Shell fire until reaching dead ground	

WAR DIARY

or

INTELLIGENCE SUMMARY.

(Erase heading not required.)

Instructions regarding War Diaries and Intelligence
Summaries are contained in F. S. Regs., Part II.
and the Staff Manual respectively. Title pages
will be prepared in manuscript.

Hour, Date, Place	Summary of Events and Information	Remarks and references to Appendices
Oct. 31st	At 10. a.m. the Bn deployed for the attack A, E, C Companies forming firing line B, C, D & H keeping local reserve while F Coy was kept as a general reserve. The Country trenches were reached under heavy shrapnel & high gun fire about 10.30 a.m. but as there was no room in the Country trenches the best cover obtainable had had to be searched for it being impossible to advance further unsupported. The Bn lay under heavy fire until dusk when the firing ceased. The trenches formed a line a little in advance of the MESSINES — WYTSCHAETE road and were not well sited. From 9 pm to 2 am the enemy made continuous attacks against our lines, all of which were unsuccessful.	The following officers were present at the action on 31st Oct (1st Nov.) Col. P.A. Malcolm Maj. R.C. Free 2nd. Mac Somanss Capt. A.H. Crawford. Lt. E.M. Stirling } A Cy 2nd Lt. P.C. Walker Capt. J.S. Cartwright } B Cy Lt. J.S. Maltby Lt. C.C. Taylor Capt. Jim Maclean } Lt. J.P. Hy. Manning } C Cy 2nd Lt. G. W. G. Matheson Lt. A. Blaikie } D Cy 2nd Lt. St. Pont 2nd Lt. R.G. Duncan } E Cy Capt. R. Brunner } Lt T.A.K. Allcot } F Capt. E.G. Mann } Lt. J.O.L. Farquharson } G Capt. J.G. C.L. Clarence } Lt. P. Paterson 2nd Lt. W.H. Anderson Capt. A. MacNab R.A.M.C. T.F

Operations of London Scottish
during 31st Oct, 1st November.

On the evening of the 30th Nov the
Bn was moved by motor transport
from YPRES and placed under
the Command of GEN GOUGH.
The battalion was without transport
or machine guns which had been
left at ST OMER under instructions
from G.H.Q About 8 am the Bn was placed under
the orders of GEN BINGHAM.
The Battalion went into action with
26 Officers and ~~500~~ 750 men. They deployed
at 10. am three Companies forming
Firing Line with supports, the windmill
¼ mile from MESSINES forming their objective.
This attack was supported by four Companies
the remaining Company being held in
reserve.
The advance ~~into place under heavy artillery~~
fire continued up to the trenches
occupied by the cavalry when owing
(b b go)

Owing to heavy artillery and machine
gun fire it was found impossible
to advance further than the trenches
already occupied by the Cavalry.
The Battalion maintained its position
until dusk when it proceeded to
Entrench as there was insufficient room
in the Cavalry trenches.
From 9pm. to the German made
Continuous but unsuccessful attacks on our lines
but at 2 am they succeeded in breaking
through on our left apparently in
large numbers. Against this force
we launched our reserve company
who with repeated bayonet charges
Succeeded in checking the advance.
This enabled the companies entrenched
in the firing line to maintain their
positions which they did until
daylight, when they discovered the

25

Germans well round both flanks.

A retirement was therefore unavoidable
and was steadily carried out under
heavy rifle and machine gun fire in
the direction of WULVERGHEM.

About 8 a.m the commanding Officer
met Gen DE LISLE who ordered him to
take up a position about
½ mile north East of WULVERGHEM, where
they remained until relieved at dusk
on the 2nd Nov.

On the night of the 1st/2nd Nov the
Bn bivouacked at LA CLYTE.

I regret to report that my casualties
are heavy, but would add that
both officers and men behaved with
great steadiness.

2nd Nov 1914

Lt Col
Commanding London Rifles

Amended list of Casualties
of Other ranks of London Scottish

Killed   14.
Wounded   122
Wounded missing 22
Missing   163   ?
               ____

Total   321
               ====

2nd Nov. 14   C.N. Campbell [?]
                   London Scottish

See further
amended list dated 6/11/14
attached

Fighting Strength of London Scottish
Before going into action 31st/1st Nov

26 Officers   786 other ranks

Fighting Strength after action

15 Officers   519 other ranks

Total Casualties.   11 Officers
                        267 other ranks.

6/11/14   C.R. Cumberbatch for R.A
                     London Scottish

30/9/14 + 1/10/14

Messines.

To Wulverghem

main attack about 3 am

XO

main attack 2 am. driven back

main attack. 2 am

3.30 am.

Reserve

A

Scottish Counter attacks about 3 am.

Wytschaete

A Position of Deployment.

Hospital

about ⅓ Wounded carried out 4 am

machine guns 6.30 am

attack by Oxfordshire Hussars + Scottish about 3 am

Trenches dug about 11 am.

To Wulverghem.

Immolation Lieut under Scottish

1/14th BATTALION

THE LONDON REGIMENT

("London Scottish"

NOVEMBER 1 9 1 4

November

Instructions regarding War Diaries and Intelligence Summaries are contained in F. S. Regs., Part II. and the Staff Manual respectively. Title pages will be prepared in manuscript.

WAR DIARY
or
INTELLIGENCE SUMMARY.
(Erase heading not required.)

Army Form C. 2118.

6

Hour, Date, Place	Summary of Events and Information	Remarks and references to Appendices
November 1st	about 2. am the German attack came pass & through our trenches and they were then driven back by our reserve company in a counter-attack. This counter attack was also assisted by a portion of C Coy who had earlier been withdrawn from the Trenches about 3. am the Germans again broke through on our left & having now no reserve company it became necessary to retire in order to avoid capture The companies in the trenches however hung on gallantly until daylight when finding themselves surrounded they fought their way out and fell back on WULVERGHEM and KEMMEL In front of KEMMEL a defensive position was maintained and at dusk the London Scottish concentrated at LA CLYTTE having been relieved in the Firing Line	During the action 31st Oct/1st Nov the rifle Mark I* have proved the very fast and nearly 50% are useless for rapid firing owing to faulty magazine. An enquiry is being made and I do expect that fresh rifles will be obtained if possible

(9 29 6) W 2794 100,000 8/14 H W V Forms/C. 2118/11.

November.

Army Form C. 2118

WAR DIARY

or

INTELLIGENCE SUMMARY.

(Erase heading not required.)

Instructions regarding War Diaries and Intelligence
Summaries are contained in F.S. Regs., Part II.
and the Staff Manual respectively. Title pages
will be prepared in manuscript.

November

Hour, Date, Place	Summary of Events and Information	Remarks and references to Appendices
Nov. 2nd	The following casualties are reported. Killed. Capt. A. Macnab RANE	
	wounded but B.Q. from. Maj. J.A. Torrance, Capt. A. MacDonald, Capt. Ross	
	Fraser. Lt. A Blackie. 2/Lt. W.H Anderson	
	under missing:- Capt. Jas. Henderson, Lt. T.M.K. Philip, Lieut.	
	J.C.L. Farquharson 3 — In Hospital sick P/t. J.C. Walker and	
	Capt. R. Drummond.	
	Other ranks. killing. 250.	
Nov 3rd	The Bn reached via LOCRE on DRANOUTRE into billets	
Nov. 4th	to mile E of BAILLEUL and joined the IX th Bde further V th Dn	14th Bde moved to YPRES
	The Bn came under the orders of St. Div. Gen. Rutland and	
	was inspected by Gen. Sir H. Smith Dorrien.	

WAR DIARY

or

INTELLIGENCE SUMMARY.

(Erase heading not required.)

Instructions regarding War Diaries and Intelligence Summaries are contained in F.S. Regs., Part II. and the Staff Manual respectively. Title pages will be prepared in manuscript.

Hour, Date, Place	Summary of Events and Information	Remarks and references to Appendices
Nov. 7th.	We left our billets about 3 pm under orders to proceed with 1st Division stores GP at STOOGE 2½ miles east of YPRES. It was dark on arriving at YPRES which was being shelled consequently we were unable to go through that town but had to billet in the road along the most. We reported to Division Hd QP about 9 pm near ULM — BELLEWAARDE FARN — sent to be quartered.	
Nov. 8th	The 1st Battalion we joined Stooge. Battalion received orders to report to before leaving ZILLEBEKE. Lt. Duncan were wounded by Shrapnel. On arrival at Hd Bde 1st QP we were sent to the wood about 1½ miles SE of ZILLEBEKE where we relieved the Sussex Regt and the 1/4th Infantry who were entrenched. Several small attacks were made on our trenches during	5 pm near the 8th when we had several infantry clearances in the wood immediately S. of HOOGE. We were headed for home. When we were sent to report to General Hd near ZILLEBEKE

WAR DIARY

or

INTELLIGENCE SUMMARY.

(Erase heading not required.)

Instructions regarding War Diaries and Intelligence Summaries are contained in F. S. Regs., Part II. and the Staff Manual respectively. Title pages will be prepared in manuscript.

Hour, Date, Place	Summary of Events and Information	Remarks and references to Appendices
Tonight 8th/9th	Our trenches were along what is known as the BRUYN ROAD. Every available man was in the trenches nor were we without any local reserves. A, B, C & E Companies were in our left trenches – their Coms the grenadier posts on the D, F, G, H. and referents by night trenches centred by 60th Rifles were E Coy, the machine guns were of the fulland E Coy and machine guns were relieved by 60th Rifles moved to our left. Three companies being on trenches A, B, C & E (from left to right). The machine guns was placed with F Coy, where flank was overlooked and often enfiladed by the Germans who held a firm immediately of there to front. Our flank to the re-enforced by men of F company and at every constant anxiety during the five days & nights spent in the trenches	J.H. Officers present at this date were / Lt.Col. G. Matthew Capt. A.S.I. CH Campbell Capt. J.H. Lindsay Capt. P.G. Clouda Capt.? P.G. Symons Lieut.? Cartwright Lieut. J. Robson Lieut. J.R. Stubbing Lieut. E.W. Stubbing Lieut. H.H.H. Normile 2Lt. R.G. Kerr-Pollard 2Lt. D.L. Frost 2Lt. C.O. Taylor 2Lt. G.H.Q. Williams Lt. J. L. Hall RAMC B.H.
November 9th		

Army Form C. 2118.

WAR DIARY

or

INTELLIGENCE SUMMARY.

(Erase heading not required.)

Instructions regarding War Diaries and Intelligence Summaries are contained in F. S. Regs., Part II. and the Staff Manual respectively. Title pages will be prepared in manuscript.

Hour, Date, Place	Summary of Events and Information	Remarks and references to Appendices
November 9th	During the day the whole line of trenches was heavily shelled. Our own Head Qrs' dug outs were blown to pieces and some of the Bn's tunnels had their dug out — only one toward Pte Cameron was badly injured though there were severely shaken. The other trenches that suffered very severely were the French ists as they had many casualties. Our actual line of trenches escaped but lives were blown down and exposed the trenches as the whole area by dusk was unrecognizable. The shelling began at 11 am straight almost 5pm. During this time the enemy infantry also attacked but were repulsed. Our Head Qrs were now moved further north and we took over those of the Grenadier Guards who were the relieving that night.	

(9 29 6) W 2794 100,000 8/14 H W V Forms/C. 2118/11.

Army Form C. 2118.

WAR DIARY

or

INTELLIGENCE SUMMARY.

(Erase heading not required.)

Instructions regarding War Diaries and Intelligence Summaries are contained in F.S. Regs., Part II. and the Staff Manual respectively. Title pages will be prepared in manuscript.

Hour, Date, Place	Summary of Events and Information	Remarks and references to Appendices
November 10	About 11 p.m. the Grenadiers were relieved by the Munster Fusiliers (Col Bent) and the Welch Regt under (Capt Reeve). The trenches originally occupied by the Grenadiers were so blown about with enemy with trees that it was deemed advisable to dig fresh trenches in rear — but this protective feature at the line ... a little which from the ... Sutton Grenadiers Sutton Scottish Welch Munsters Scottish From Nov 8th to 13th we were constantly heavily shelled and attacked in varying degrees by night and day. The position was one of continual anxiety more especially with regard to our right flank where we lost some 25 to 30 men on the 10th 2/Lt Fulland was hit and Sgt Smart was being buried killed by a shell	Approximate place of 2/Lt Fulland. N.W. corner of the field one mile W. of YPRES on the YPRES - VLAMERTINGHE Road. Nov 1534 Capt K.C. MacDonald was also (killed) ... 2/Lt Fulland died in hospital grounds ... buried in a field near YPRES on the 12th.

(9 29 6) W 2794 100,000 8/14 H W V Forms/C. 2118/11.

WAR DIARY

or

INTELLIGENCE SUMMARY.

(*Erase heading not required.*)

Instructions regard☐ War Diaries and Intelligence
Summaries are contained in F.S. Regs., Part II.
and the Staff Manual respectively. Title pages
will be prepared in manuscript.

Hour, Date, Place	Summary of Events and Information	Remarks and references to Appendices
On 13ᵗʰ Nov.	From the 8ᵗʰ to 13ᵗʰ we lost in killed and wounded 2 officers and about 70 men.	
	About 11 p.m. on the 13ᵗʰ we were relieved by Cavalry and marched back through ZILLEBEKE (forward immediately S. of Hooge on the YPRES — MENIN road.	
	As there were dug outs available on arrival here we slept as well as we could as the guns fired all over us during the night.	
	Men Killed during 13ᵗʰ Nov. [ ] Capt. J. H. Rutton was	
14ᵗʰ Nov.	Dug outs on the 14ᵗʰ Nov. hit by shattered shrapnel.	☐. E. Scott
	On the 14ᵗʰ we were placed as Corps Reserve under the 1ˢᵗ Bde & that time commanded by Col. J. Green.	
	Officers Camerons [the Brigadier found Intelligence had been Killed 2 days previously. The 1ˢᵗ Bde cavalry Self fronts Black Watch, Camerons ourselves.]	
15ᵗʰ Nov.	Still acting as Corps Reserve	

Army Form C. 2118.

WAR DIARY

or

INTELLIGENCE SUMMARY.

(Erase heading not required.)

Instructions regarding War Diaries and Intelligence Summaries are contained in F. S. Regs., Part II. and the Staff Manual respectively. Title pages will be prepared in manuscript.

Hour, Date, Place	Summary of Events and Information	Remarks and references to Appendices
16th Nov.	The 1st Bn moved at ... am to new billets 16th via YPRES VLAMERTINGE to WESTOUTRE where they ... during the night of the 16/17th.	Scott X
17th Nov	... the 17th at 9.30 am the Bn marched via LOCRE and BAILLEUL to BORRE STRAZEELE and BORRE.	
19th Nov.	The Bn arrived ... has moved from BORRE to ... The Bn ... has moved from BORRE to PRADELLES ... from BORRE ... Saturday [NTH Prince Charles ... 1st Div inspected the Bn... Gen Landon commanding (1st Div inspected the Bn. Col ... (Brig.) inspected transport)	
20th Nov. 21st		
22nd	Mr Vallance held a Divine Service in church at PRADELLES	
23rd	Maj General Sir David Henderson made to relieve Gen Landon Visited ... R.R. There is finally refitting but is slow in getting over its recent fighting	

Army Form C. 2118.

Instructions regarding War Diaries and Intelligence
Summaries are contained in F. S. Regs., Part II.
and the Staff Manual respectively. Title pages
will be prepared in manuscript.

WAR DIARY
or
INTELLIGENCE SUMMARY.
(Erase heading not required.)

Hour, Date, Place	Summary of Events and Information	Remarks and references to Appendices
23rd Nov	The command of the 1st 113th Bde taken over by Col E.H.C. Forster C.B.O. C.H.G. D.S.o	
25th. Nov	The following officers proceeded on 120 hours leave England Col Malcolm, Capt Clowes. Lieut Robertson, Lieut Stothert 2/Lt Taylor. Col Malcolm was granted further leave by medical board held in England. Captain Stephenson E.T. Campbell took over temporary command of the battalion	
Nov. 28th	Field Marshal Sir John French visited the battalion and complimented officers NCOs men on their recent fighting	
	A draft of 5 officers and 187 other ranks arrived from England. The officers were Captain C Gour. Captain G N Ford 2/Lt G P Mackinnon, Lt N Ramsay Mackie, 2/Lt N W Tait 2/Lt Waller rejoined the Bn from hospital antenna appended Transport officer	Draft 5 Officers 187 — Other Ranks
Nov. 29th	Church parade which was attended by Col Sr Brisson & B.J.e.	
Nov. 30th	Officers granted 120 hours leave on the 25th returned unit there afternoon of Col Malcolm. Rear 2/Lt Vallance Lt Sgt. Stirling, Lt H.H. Mercylin were granted leave to proceed to England until 9 pm on 4th Dec.	1000 Strength of Bn at this date 17 officers 814 other ranks

(9 29 6) W 2794 100,000 8/14 H W V Forms/C. 2118/11.

Army Form C. 2121.

"A"
MESSAGES AND SIGNALS.

No. of Message

C Code | Words | Charge
e of Origin and Service Instructions.

This message is on a/c of

Recd. at

Sent

Date

At | m.

Service.

From

To

By

(Signature of "Franking Officer.")

By

TO —
South Wales Borders   number

B.R.R.

London Scottish

Sender's Number | Day of Month | In reply to Number | A A A

BM/834 | 12th

Following received from 1st Corps
"Begins" Prisoners state that the
"German Guard Reg^ts were brought
"up to relieve their XXVII Corps and
"were told to make ~~supreme~~
"supreme effort yesterday to break
"through as their other Corps had
"failed add French reinforcements
"are at hand and everything
"depends on our holding our
"positions today" Message ends
add Please report situation
in front of you in order
that I may direct artillery
in most effective places

From Lord Cavan

Place

Time

The above may be forwarded as now corrected. | (Z)

W. Rüttmer Major

Censor. | Signature of Addressor or person authorised to telegraph in his name

*This line should be erased if not required.

8562 M. & Co. Ltd. Wt. W922/549—100,000. 5/14. Forms C2121/10.

1/14th BATTALION

THE LONDON REGIMENT

"London Scottish"

DECEMBER 1 9 1 4

December

Erskine Scotter

Army Form C. 2118

WAR DIARY

or

INTELLIGENCE SUMMARY.

(Erase heading not required.)

Instructions regarding War Diaries and Intelligence Summaries are contained in F.S. Regs., Part II. and the Staff Manual respectively. Title pages will be prepared in manuscript.

Hour, Date, Place	Summary of Events and Information	Remarks and references to Appendices
December 3rd	The 1st Bn lined either side of the road east of BORRE for the visit of His Majesty the King. H.M. the King and the Prince of Wales went & walked down between the two lines of the Rankin Scottah accompanied by C.O. Capt Campbell who was temporarily in command. His majesty informed the Commanding Officer his pleasure at the appearance of the men and congratulated the state of the post work done by the regiment in the field.	H.R.H. The Prince of Wales was also present.
Dec. 4th	Route Marching, Neuve Eglise. Returned after 10.8 hours.	Capt our Adjutant Lt Campbell having on the command of the Battalion to Capt (temporary Major) P.W. Sandilands DSO Commanding on Monday 7th Dec.
Dec. 5th	No. 2159 P & O. which both H.Q. and 2/86 Pte Capt H. Kitchin left the battalion State Commission in the Bienvenu Stephro	
Dec. 6th	Church Parade. Capt P.C.K. Christie left for England on 7	Present strength 18 Officers 609 other Ranks
Dec. 7th-8th	Cage Team under Lieut Hern his sight attested Capt Cranmith headed are Command of the Battalion 6 Capt (temp Maj) P W Sandilands DSO in new. 1st line of drainage & canine.	
9.	No. 2067 Pte W. T. Murray A Coy left for England to take up a temporary Commission in the Regiment Army (9th London Regt)	

Forms/C. 2118/11.

(9 29 6) W 2794 100,000 8/14 H W V

Army Form C. 2118

7.

WAR DIARY

or

INTELLIGENCE SUMMARY.

(*Erase heading not required.*)

Instructions regarding War Diaries and Intelligence
Summaries are contained in F. S. Regs., Part II.
and the Staff Manual respectively. Title pages
will be prepared in manuscript.

Hour, Date, Place	Summary of Events and Information	Remarks and references to Appendices
December Sunday 20th	left PRADELLES 5pm and marched into STRAZEELE MERVILLE to BETHUNE, arriving 1.30AM Billeted in the Theatre.	Lon. Scot.
Monday 21st	Marched 12 noon via BEUVRY to near CUINCHY arriving 2.30pm. 1st Brigade attached to action around GIVANCHY at 2.45 PM. The Coldstream Guards and 1st Cameron Highlanders formed the firing line — Scots Guards Reserve — London Scottish and Black Watch 2nd line; attack developed about 3.30pm. Scots Guards were put on right of attack N. of Canal. The Germans were cleared out of GIVANCHY and Coldstream Guards, Cameron Highlanders and Scots Guards held their trenches. At 7.30 pm. No 1 Coy London Scottish was sent to fill a gap on the right of the Coldstream Guards. At 11.30 P.M. No 2 Coy was sent out to Patrol the North	

(9 29 6)   W 2794   100,000   8/14   H W V   Forms/C. 2118/11.

18.

WAR DIARY
or
INTELLIGENCE SUMMARY.

(Erase heading not required.)

Instructions regarding War Diaries and Intelligence Summaries are contained in F. S. Regs., Part II. and the Staff Manual respectively. Title pages will be prepared in manuscript.

Hour, Date, Place	Summary of Events and Information	Remarks and references to Appendices
Tuesday, 23ᵈ	bank of the Canal but returned in about 3 hours.	L. Scott
	At 2.30 AM ½ N°3 Coy went forward to lengthen the line on the left of the Cameronians and ½ further left to continue the French line.	
	At 10 AM the machine guns went up to the Coldstream Guards.	
	At 1 PM the 6.6. and N°2 Coy went up to fill the gap between our right and the French line.	
	At 3.30 PM the Adjutant and N°1 Coy which had previously been withdrawn went up on the left of the line	
	At 8.30 P.M. the machine guns, N°2 Coy, N°3 Coy and two platoons N°4 were relieved by the Royal Berkshire Regiment	
	Captain G.N. York was wounded	
23ʳᵈ	3 Platoons N°4 Coy and N°1 Coy were relieved by N°2 Coy.	
	Captain H.C. Cartwright was wounded.	
	The machine guns were relieved by the Scots Guards.	

Army Form C. 2118.

WAR DIARY

or

INTELLIGENCE SUMMARY.

(Erase heading not required.)

Instructions regarding War Diaries and Intelligence
Summaries are contained in F. S. Regs., Part II.
and the Staff Manual respectively. Title pages
will be prepared in manuscript.

Hour, Date, Place	Summary of Events and Information	Remarks and references to Appendices
	(Lieutenant A. G. Stebbing took over Command of No. 4 from Captain Ford (wounded)	
24th	No. 2 Company was relieved by No. 3 Coy about 9 PM and the Machine guns relieved those of the 4th Scots Guards. Lieutenant So. Combat Taylor took over Command of No. 1 Coy. Major Sandilands went to Hospital with rheumatism.	Low. Scott
25th	Captain and Adjutant G. H. Campbell took over Command of the Battalion from Major W. Sandilands. D.S.O. and Lieutenant J. Paterson took on the duties of Adjutant. No. 4 Company relieved No. 3 Coy about 8.30 P.M. No. 1 Company went to the Redoubt in Reserve less one Platoon.	
26th	No. 1 Company relieved No. 3 less one Platoon. No. 2 Company relieved No. 1 Coy.	
27th	12-25 PM Head Quarters and Companies billetted had to stand by for an expected attack which a German deserter said would take place. This was a false alarm.	

(9 29 6)   W 2794   100,000   8/14   H W V   Forms/C. 2118/11.

WAR DIARY
or
INTELLIGENCE SUMMARY.

(Erase heading not required.)

Instructions regarding War Diaries and Intelligence Summaries are contained in F.S. Regs., Part II. and the Staff Manual respectively. Title pages will be prepared in manuscript.

Hour, Date, Place	Summary of Events and Information	Remarks and references to Appendices
28th.	No 2 Coy relieves No 1 Coy, No 3 relieves No 2.	
	"The O.C. London Scottish"	
	The following is a copy of a message received this day from Brig. Gen. H.C. Lowther, Commanding 1st Guards Brigade.	
	"It is now only a short time since the London Scottish on church parade	for Scott
	"made some remarks to the London Scottish on church parade	
	"relating to the spirit of the battalion."	
	"I wish to say how very satisfactory the present state	
	"of the battalion appeals to be and with what confidence	
	"I look forward to your future performances"	
	"This shews that you to a General Henderson's remarks	
	"in the spirit in which they were meant.	
	"In the past few days the country has to thank	
	"the courage and humanity of several of your number	
	"for the lives of wounded who saved by your efforts.	
	"The G.O.C. Commanding the Division has been informed	

(0 29 6) W 2794 100,000 8/14 H W V   Forms/C. 2118/11.

Army Form C. 2118

WAR DIARY
or
INTELLIGENCE SUMMARY.

(Erase heading not required.)

Instructions regarding War Diaries and Intelligence Summaries are contained in F. S. Regs., Part II. and the Staff Manual respectively. Title pages will be prepared in manuscript.

Hour, Date, Place	Summary of Events and Information	Remarks and references to Appendices
	"of this, as well as of the excellent military spirit which "has pervaded you. "We had have had times to go through together, "but I confidently trust the London Scottish to be up to "any call made upon them." (Signed) H.C. Lowther Brig. Gen. Commanding 1st Guards Brigade.	Lon Scott
28/11/14.	Re. Lieut Lidort - Machines and gun teams relieved teams of Cameron Highlanders in "Scottish Trench" about 5-30 PM. At 6-30 PM. No 4 Coy joined No 3 Coy in its 1st Reserve Redoubt. 2596 Pte PG Hill, 3157 Pte G. Lawrence and 2322 Pte J.B. Monro left for St. OMER in order to attend a Machine Gun Course. The 1st Brigade less London Scottish and Black Watch	

(6) W 2794 100,000 8/14 H W V   Forms/C. 2118/11.

WAR DIARY
or
INTELLIGENCE SUMMARY.

(*Erase heading not required.*)

Instructions regarding War Diaries and Intelligence
Summaries are contained in F. S. Regs., Part II.
and the Staff Manual respectively. Title pages
will be prepared in manuscript.

Hour, Date, Place	Summary of Events and Information	Remarks and references to Appendices
	marched to BETHUNE for a rest about 5 P.M. N° 2 Coy London Scottish were relieved by Black Watch at 4-50 P.M.	see text
	The Black Watch took over the main line of Trenches, and both Black Watch and London Scottish were attached to the 2nd Brigade.	
29th	N°s 1 and N°s 2 Companies occupied 1st Reserve (Redoubt)	
30th	The whole Battalion moved into the Trenches, relieving the Black Watch as follows :—	
	FRENCH FARM. 158 men at 4 P.M.	
	SCOTTISH TRENCH. 95 men at 4-30 P.M.	
	WAGON TRENCH. 50 men at 5 P.M.	
	Right Section MAIN TRENCH. 40 men at 5 P.M.	
	The remainder in reserve;	
	The Battalion Head Quarters & billets were taken over by the Black Watch.	

(9 29 6) W 2794 100,000 8/14 H W V   Forms/C. 2118/11.

Copy

31st December 1914

Platoons of the Companies in the Trenches were relieved in turn and brought into shelter in armed houses for periods of not less than 12 hours each.

A scheme of improvement of the trenches was initiated and the work began

LONDON SCOTTISH

(14TH LONDON REGT)

JAN - DEC 1915

1st Division.

1st Brigade

W A R   D I A R Y

L O N D O N   S C O T T I S H
(14th London Regiment.)

January

1 9 1 5

Army Form C. 21

WAR DIARY

or

INTELLIGENCE SUMMARY.

(Erase heading not required.)

Instructions regarding War Diaries and Intelligence Summaries are contained in F.S. Regs., Part II. and the Staff Manual respectively. Title pages will be prepared in manuscript.

Hour, Date, Place	Summary of Events and Information	Remarks and references to Appendices
31st December	Platoons of the Companies in the trenches were relieved in turn and brought into shelter in huts and homes for periods of not less than 12 hours each. A scheme of improvement of the trenches was initiated and the work begun	J. 5
1st January	One hour before midnight on the 31st very heavy rifle and gun fire began on both sides to herald the New Year. Organisation of 8 of the best shots in the Battalion to act as snipers was considered both the object of stalking the German snipers. 1st Brigade returned from rest. Battalion bivouaced. Battalion from the 10th Reserve Battalion	OK
2nd January		
3rd January		
4th January	A system of reliefs explained under 31st December has been worked extremely well, 2 Platoons only having been in the trenches without relief for longer than 48 hours.	

Army Form C. 2118

WAR DIARY
or
INTELLIGENCE SUMMARY.
(Erase heading not required.)

Instructions regarding War Diaries and Intelligence Summaries are contained in F. S. Regs., Part II. and the Staff Manual respectively. Title pages will be prepared in manuscript.

Hour, Date, Place	Summary of Events and Information	Remarks and references to Appendices
	During all this time men had hot stew supported brought up by the Reserve Platoons from d'hout about half a mile from the trenches, called "windy corner" which reached them about 6-30 P.M and again hot tea about 4 A.M. In practically every case this food was still stolen it reached the men actually in the trenches. Observations hood, hand-bombs, grenades etc were brought up to within 300 yards of the Trenches by the pack horses both embossed Renniers No 1 and 3 companies moved into Reserve at CUINCHY, No 2 into Church Reserve, at Pont d'aphni about 300 yards from the trenches leaving N? Company in French Farm, the remainder of the line held by us during the last 5 days being taken over by the BLACK WATCH. Machine Gun also goes into Church Reserve.	£5

(9 29 6) W 2794 100,000 8/14 H W V Forms/C. 2118/11.

Army Form C. 21.

WAR DIARY

or

INTELLIGENCE SUMMARY.

(Erase heading not required.)

Instructions regarding War Diaries and Intelligence Summaries are contained in F. S. Regs., Part II. and the Staff Manual respectively. Title pages will be prepared in manuscript.

Hour, Date, Place	Summary of Events and Information	Remarks and references to Appendices
5th January	No 2 and 4 Companies change Places	J.S.
6th January	No 2 and 4 Companies go into Reserve. No 1 and	
	3 move up, No 3 to trench farm and No 1 to Reserve.	
	Machine Gun goes to SCOTTISH trench on the left of -	
7th January	Trench farm. On this day the MINENWERFER was first reported.	
	23rd Field Company R.E.	
	No 1 and 3 change over	
	improve Church Reserve, by making loop-holes, putting	
	the Place in a state of defence, putting wire into entangle-	
	ments outside, leaving an entrance a short under-	
	ground passage approached by a steep flight of -	
	steps at either end.	

(9 29 6) W 2794 100,000 8/13 H W V Forms/C. 2118/11.

Army Form C. 21?.

Instructions regarding War Diaries and Intelligence
Summaries are contained in F.S. Regs., Part II.
and the Staff Manual respectively. Title pages
will be prepared in manuscript.

WAR DIARY
or
INTELLIGENCE SUMMARY.

(Erase heading not required.)

26.

Hour, Date, Place	Summary of Events and Information	Remarks and references to Appendices
8th January	No 1 and 3 Companies go into reserve at GUINCHY Nos 2 and 4 come up to trench lines and 2 to Church Reserve. Machine Guns were relieved.	1 5
9th January	No 1 and 4 charge over. A few were artillery. Duel was commenced by the British. No advantage ceased to rest decidedly with us.	
10 January	No 1 plus one Platoon of No 3 and Machine Guns go into trench farm; the remainder of No 3 in Church Reserve. No 2 had a Platoon of No 2 in Reserve at PNT FIXE, the remainder in Billets.	(W)
	A Platoon of the Reserve was called on by the Scots Guards but was not used.	
11th January	~~crossed out text~~	

(9 29 6)   W 2794   100,000   8/14   H W V   Forms/C. 2118/11.

WAR DIARY

or

INTELLIGENCE SUMMARY.

(*Erase heading not required.*)

Instructions regarding War Diaries and Intelligence Summaries are contained in F. S. Regs., Part II. and the Staff Manual respectively. Title pages will be prepared in manuscript.

Hour, Date, Place	Summary of Events and Information	Remarks and references to Appendices
11th January	Church Parade "Am told the Battalion went out in Church Reserve was relieved by the Coldstreamers about 4 P.M. and the remainder of the Battalion by the Queens and moved into Billets at BEUVRY	
12th January	The Battalion moved into BETHUNE and was billetted at the ORPHANAGE and became Corps Troops finding several Guards etc	L. S.
13th January	Spent in cleaning	
14th January	Remainder of 4th BRIGADE came to rest at BETHUNE. BRIG. GEN. LOWTHER 1st GUARDS BRIGADE inspected Billets	CW
15th January	and expressed himself as very pleased. All men of the Bn hit on duty had an official bath under N.C.R.A.M.C at the Hospital. The arrangements here excellent. all clothing being disinfected.	
16th January	The 91 A. 9 M.P.S inspected the Billets The Bn gave a Concert in the MAIRIE at BETHUNE.	

WAR DIARY

or

INTELLIGENCE SUMMARY.

(Erase heading not required.)

Instructions regarding War Diaries and Intelligence
Summaries are contained in F. S. Regs., Part II.
and the Staff Manual respectively. Title pages
will be prepared in manuscript.

Hour, Date, Place	Summary of Events and Information	Remarks and references to Appendices
17th January	GEN MUNRO Commanding First Corps was present. Captain C.H. Crawshell and Lieutenant Quartermaster W.G. Webb having left for ENGLAND on the night of the 16th Captain Grave assumes command of the Battalion.	
18th January	2912 Sergeant Major A. Grant proceeds to ENGLAND to-day to join the First Reserve Battalion.	J.S.
	3485 Sergeant Major W.C. Smith joins the Battalion to day from the First Reserve Battalion.	
20th Jany	Captain C.H. Crawshell Captain W. Scott returned from leave. Lieutenant Stuart Sinclair	D.W.
	The Battalion was Inspected by Major General R.C.B. HAKING, C.B. Commanding First Division.	
21st January	The Battalion marched to CUINCHY relieving the NORTHAMPTON regiment in the trenches our left resting on the LA BASSÉE Canal with the Cameron Highlanders extending from our right to the LA BASSÉE — BÉTHUNE ROAD.	

WAR DIARY
or
INTELLIGENCE SUMMARY
(Erase heading not required.)

Instructions regarding War Diaries and Intelligence Summaries are contained in F. S. Regs., Part II. and the Staff Manual respectively. Title pages will be prepared in manuscript.

Hour, Date, Place	Summary of Events and Information	Remarks and references to Appendices
22 January	Quiet – some shelling	
23 January	Battalion was relieved at dusk by 1st Coldstream Guards. Casualties during day 2 Killed, 3 wounded of whom 1 died of wounds on 27th Instant	
24th January	The Battalion went into Billets at CAMBRIN ¾ mile behind trenches. Day spent in cleaning, shaving etc.	J. S.
25 January	At 7-30 AM the Battalion was sent to reinforce the 4th Guards and Coldstream Guards who had been driven from their trenches by a heavy German attack. The Battalion arrived at CUINCHY church under fairly heavy shell fire but with only one or two casualties. No 4 Coy (Lt HG Stirling) and 2 Platoons No 2 Coy (Lt O'Brien) were sent forward to occupy ground N.E. of CUINCHY CHURCH supporting what was left of the Scots GUARDS. This movement also was able to watch and move towards the La BASSÉE Road that night to be made by the Germans.	

1247 W 3299 200,000 (E) 8/14 J.B.C. & A. Forms/C. 2118/11.

'WAR DIARY

or

INTELLIGENCE SUMMARY

(Erase heading not required.)

Instructions regarding War Diaries and Intelligence Summaries are contained in F. S. Regs., Part II. and the Staff Manual respectively. Title pages will be prepared in manuscript.

Hour, Date, Place	Summary of Events and Information	Remarks and references to Appendices
25 January (Contd)	One machine Gun under 2/Lt Lindsay hatto was placed in the upper storey of a house 80 yards N.E. of Cuinchy Churchyard to this home 8 of the Battalion snipers were also sent. These both the machine Gun did good work throughout the day At 1 P.M. the 1st BLACK WATCH and 60th RIFLES (from BETHUNE) were sent to make a counterattack This was done but was not very successfully carried out. At 5 P.M. No 1 Coy under Captain Tyler was sent to assist the BLACK WATCH near PUDDING LANE. At 7 P.M. the SUSSEX Regt made a counterattack which had little effect In spite of these unsuccessful counterattacks the enemy gained no hore ground and the net result of the day's work was a gain of about 30 yards along a front of 3/4 mile Casualties on both sides heavy. Our own casualties here small – 2 killed and 10 wounded. About 12 midnight Major B.C. Green arrived and rejoined the Battalion, taking over command from	

1247 W 8299 200,000 (E) 8/14 J.B.C. & A.   Forms/C. 2118/11.

Army Form C. 2118.

WAR DIARY
or
INTELLIGENCE SUMMARY

(Erase heading not required.)

Instructions regarding War Diaries and Intelligence Summaries are contained in F. S. Regs, Part II. and the Staff Manual respectively. Title pages will be prepared in manuscript.

Hour, Date, Place	Summary of Events and Information	Remarks and references to Appendices
25th January (Contd)	Captain C.H. Campbell in the early hours of the morning of the 26th January.	J.S
26th January	At 1 A.M. the Battalion was ordered back to CAMBRIN, leaving No. 1 Coy. still in the trenches under command of O.C. BLACK WATCH. This Company was relieved and rejoined its Battalion about 4 P.M. The day was spent in constant readiness to return to the trenches but at 2 P.M. orders were received that the Battalion would go back to BETHUNE. At 7 P.M. the Battalion moved to BETHUNE when it arrived about 8-45 P.M. The following officers joined the Battalion — Captain J.H. Ross, 2/Lt. J.B. Snell, 2/Lt. W. McScott.	
27th - 31st January	The Battalion has been in constant readiness to march back to the trenches as very heavy fighting was taking place between those dates, but during this period the Germans had heavy without any real success.	OKC

1247 W 3299 200,000 (E) 8/14 J.B.C.&A. Forms/C. 2118/11.

1st Division.

1st Brigade

WAR DIARY

LONDON SCOTTISH

(14th London Regiment.)

February

1 9 1 5

Army Form C. 2118.

WAR DIARY

or

INTELLIGENCE SUMMARY

(Erase heading not required.)

Instructions regarding War Diaries and Intelligence Summaries are contained in F. S. Regs., Part II. and the Staff Manual respectively. Title pages will be prepared in manuscript.

Hour, Date, Place	Summary of Events and Information	Remarks and references to Appendices
1st February 1915	Battalion in Brigade Reserve at BETTHUNE. 7AM Column bivouac to 1RE PREOL no reserve to 3rd Brigade. Remains near railway Culvert all day bivouac track to BETHUNE at 6.30 PM	J Scott
2nd February	The Battalion move from BETTHUNE with Rest first at 6AM onwards into a rest camp at HURIONVILLE near LILLERS.	
3rd February	A thorough Scheme of Training was commenced under instruction for 1st Bn. Appointments & Rewards. C.S.M. T.C. Wood Sgt E.J. Findlay Pte J.A. Brown-Constable Pte K.H. Marshall Capt J.A. J Macfarlanes	J.A. Brown-Constable Sgt K.H. Marshall
5th February	Court of enquiry with two of prisoners at CAMBRIN. Readers Corps dyer : Senders the 7/5 dated 7/1/15 dated 17/1/15 Lieut London Gazette 11/7/14	
6th Feby.	Sgt A.H. Macfargot promotion & 2/Lt he was posted to A Coy	
7th Feby.	The following message was received from 1st Division by 1.st Brigade :- "Commander in Chief wishes me to express to you his appreciation of the excellent work done by the troops under your command during the past six weeks"	
9th February	The following Officers have proceeded to England in ill health under the dates stated against their names:- 2/Lt C. Cringat Taylor 3/2/15 Lt T.F. Hill	Lt M.E. Sketching 7/1/16 2/Lt J.C. Walker 26/1/15 2/Lt A.H. Macfargot 2/Lt J.A. J Macfarlane 9/2/15
	2/Lt T.C. Wood Lt E.J. Findlay Pte J.C. Brown-Constable Lt K.H. Marshall	

1247 W 3299 200,000 (E) 8/14 J.B.C. & A. Forms/C. 2118/11.

WAR DIARY
or
INTELLIGENCE SUMMARY

(Erase heading not required.)

Instructions regarding War Diaries and Intelligence
Summaries are contained in F. S. Regs., Part II.
and the Staff Manual respectively. Title pages
will be prepared in manuscript.

Hour, Date, Place	Summary of Events and Information	Remarks and references to Appendices
11th February 1915	The G.O.C. 1st Div. inspected the billets and expressed himself well satisfied.	
	S.7. Maj. W.C. Smith assumes command & administration for Brunn. McC. in Battalion till Major Duthie re-	
12th	Major J.F.H. Hamilton D.S.O. Blackheath took over command of the Bn. from Brig Gen J.F.C. fourth handover.	
	Police force & new companies Shut cause of air machine in the use of French mortars. Bombs under the 26th Bde R.F.A. —	
15th	2.3 Field Company R.E. respectively. Lt Col C.E. Stewart Blackheath took over command of the brigade on return from leave.	J. Sec
19th February	Brig Gen Lt Col. W. Lowe Reg. are attached for infantry duties under a R.A.F.C.T. Roach.	
20th February	Brig Gen McC took returns from leave and resumed command of the Brigade.	
21st February	Shute's battalion has billets at the RAIMBERT COLLIERY	
21st to 24th February	The Commanding Officer inspects Companies in marching order	
22nd February	Capt F.C.K. Clowes rejoined and Lt R. Crew & Capts H. Buchanan, J.L. Duncan	
23rd	T.D. Duncan joined the Bn from the 1st Reserve	
24th Feby	Captains —Asi. McCarthy — Capt Mgr Lt W.E. Webb. Left England on Short Leave. Lt J. Paterson R.V.E. Starting in from their duties respectively	
	Major R.C. Green T.D. Commanding in from the R.H.Q. dating 16th Feby.	
27th Feby	The battalion was inspected by Major C.G. Munro of a 1st Army Corps.	
28th February	The battalion moves from SHURLONVILLE & Billets near SAILLY. billets at the 13th Bn. 3rd Brigade Reg. 1st line Transport in Stalingrad LE TOURET	

1st Division.

1st Brigade

WAR   DIARY

LONDON   SCOTTISH

(14th London Regiment.)

March

1 9 1 5

WAR DIARY

or

INTELLIGENCE SUMMARY

(*Erase heading not required.*)

Instructions regarding War Diaries and Intelligence
Summaries are contained in F. S. Regs., Part II.
and the Staff Manual respectively. Title pages
will be prepared in manuscript.

Hour, Date, Place	Summary of Events and Information	Remarks and references to Appendices
March		
1st	Battalion in Brigade Reserve at EPINETTE. Seals to occupy works E2,3,3 and 5 in the event of standing to arms. [Fatigue Party went out at night to military the trenches at BREWERY Post. Casualties, (Lieut ____ killed)]	$\int S$
2nd	At night Capt D Coy [under Captain E.C.?] relieved the CAMERONS at BREWERY Post. They were under the orders of O.C, 1st Bn's BURGE. Lieut Colonel C.C. to Stewart. BLACK WATCH took over command of 1st BRIGADE.	
3rd	Captain and Adjutant C.H Campbell and Captain ____ Lieutenants, etc. both returned from short leave and took over their duties from Lieut ____ Paterson and Captain H.B. Stirling respectively.	
4th	Cand D Companies were relieved at night by the CAMERONS. The Halkirk Tram has been promoted and it went out in the trenches Sept of the Brigade line near CHOCOLAT MENIER Corner.	c.a.Cmr
5th	Brigadier General H.C GUNTHER resumed command of the Brigade. Attacked by the enemy bombardment as they had been Kennery trenches [in front of their defence along the RUE DE CAILLAUX some firing at night but was quickly silenced by the Brigade Artillery. Divisional Battalion HeadQuarters	
6th	7 A.B Coys. [under Captain H.L. Legg] relieved the CAMERONS at BREWERY Post.	
7th	Two bursts of bombardment at 11 P.M. and 2 A.M. to cover a	

WAR DIARY

or

INTELLIGENCE SUMMARY

(Erase heading not required.)

Instructions regarding War Diaries and Intelligence Summaries are contained in F. S. Regs., Part II. and the Staff Manual respectively. Title pages will be prepared in manuscript.

Hour, Date, Place	Summary of Events and Information	Remarks and references to Appendices
	French attack on the right. Vicinity of Battalion Headquarters shelled by shrapnel.	
8th.	A and B Companies were relieved.	
9th.	Message from Sir Douglas HAIG G.O.C. 1st Army that the British line was in a position to advance on the left. Captain R Brereve and Lieut to Brunet Taylor went to Hospital.	J. S
10th.	Very severe bombardment of NEUVE CHAPELLE. At night Scots GUARDS and LONDON SCOTTISH were moved G.RICHEBOURG A VAAST and the Irish Regiment to Rouen billets. Reinforcement was cancelled and the Battalion returned to their barracks billets.	(M.G.A.A?)
11th.	Enemy reported to be massing for an attack at CHOCOLAT MENIER Corner. Every available man ready to turn out. Attack did not take place.	
12th-13th.	C and D Coys and 30 men of B 36 (150 rifles in all) went to Left flank at BREWERY Post under Captain G. of Clowes. Severe shelling of EPINETTE by the Germans.	
14th.	Arrival of Draft Lieut A.A. Harrington and Lieut W.A. Anderson. Reinforced and Lieut to Robertson joined the Battalion. 128 Other Ranks.	

1247 W 3299 200,000 (E) 8/14 J.B.C. & A. Forms/C. 2118/11.

WAR DIARY

or

INTELLIGENCE SUMMARY

(Erase heading not required.)

Instructions regarding War Diaries and Intelligence
Summaries are contained in F. S. Regs., Part II.
and the Staff Manual respectively. Title pages
will be prepared in manuscript.

Hour, Date, Place	Summary of Events and Information	Remarks and references to Appendices
15th	from ENGLAND and then Festival Base, ROUEN also joined. The draft was inspected by the Commanding Officer. Germans shelled C and D Companies, Billets and then their redoubts bombing them.	
16th	From 5 P.M. till 2 P.M. 16th they sent 80 high explosive shells in the vicinity of Battalion Headquarters. Orderly Room hit by shell and 3 Telegraphists wounded; also Captain and Adjutant C.A. (and Nell and several villages to South (3685) slightly wounded. Both remain with their unit.	
17th	Germans again shelled Battalion Headquarters which were moved. Lieutenant R. H. Marshall was accidentally wounded. /leaves to TOURET	
18th	BRIGADIER GEN. H.C. LOWTHER visited Headquarters. At night Companies came out. 3 Casualties occurred. Battalion was in Brigade Reserve, ready to move at very short notice.	
20th	Companies returned to BREWERY POST	
21st	Good work by Battalion Snipers and Rifled Shots.	
22nd	Headquarters again severely shelled; 2 Casualties. Moved to from 500 yards away, which was also shelled.	

1247 W 3299 200,000 (E) 8/14 J.B.C. & A. Forms/C. 2118/11.

WAR DIARY

or

INTELLIGENCE SUMMARY

(Erase heading not required.)

Instructions regarding War Diaries and Intelligence Summaries are contained in F. S. Regs, Part II. and the Staff Manual respectively. Title pages will be prepared in manuscript.

Hour, Date, Place	Summary of Events and Information	Remarks and references to Appendices
22 (cont.)	Battalion relieved at night by 9th Bn H.L.I. (Glasgow Highlanders) and late at night it marched to VENDIN-LEZ-BETHUNE where it billeted. A new draft of 292 Other Ranks has been joining there (249 from ENGLAND and 23 returned from ROUEN)	
	During the last three weeks both the Germans and ourselves occupied defences guarded by sand-bags and earth works, the ground being too flat and wet to allow of trenches being dug. Our works took the form of "Some Butts" containing 20 or 30 men and placed at intervals of 100 yards.	
24th	At 4 P.M. marched [from VENDIN to very near to] [billets near] HINGES and LOCON.	
25th	New drafts inspected by Brig. Gen. H.C Lowther.	
26th	New drafts inspected by Major Gen. R.C.B Haking, G.O.C 1st Division	
27th	2/Lieut. J.C. Brown - Constable went sick to Hospital.	
28th	The Battalion was in Brigade working and on duty.	
30th	The Battalion moved off at 3-30 P.M. and marched [via LE TOURET]	

Army Form C. 2118.

WAR DIARY

or

INTELLIGENCE SUMMARY

(Erase heading not required.)

Instructions regarding War Diaries and Intelligence
Summaries are contained in F. S. Regs., Part II.
and the Staff Manual respectively. Title pages
will be prepared in manuscript.

Hour, Date, Place	Summary of Events and Information	Remarks and references to Appendices
30th (cont.)	to RUE DE L'EPINETTE where it remained about 4.30 P.M. + taken from the Expeditionary Regiment. A and B Coys under Captain W[?] took over the defences at Indian Village. Battalion Headquarters were situated in RUE DE L'EPINETTE near the R.E. Store.	
31st	A quiet day. One slight casualty reported from the Butts. Defences at Indian Village improved both day and corrugated iron. A fatigue party reported to R.E.'s line. Other improvement carried on at night.	

1247 W 3299 200,000 (E) 8/14 J.B.C. & A. Forms/C. 2118/11.

WAR
DIARY

LONDON SCOTTISH

(14th London Regiment)

A P R I L

1 9 1 5

WAR DIARY
or
INTELLIGENCE SUMMARY

(Erase heading not required.)

Instructions regarding War Diaries and Intelligence Summaries are contained in F. S. Regs., Part II. and the Staff Manual respectively. Title pages will be prepared in manuscript.

Hour, Date, Place	Summary of Events and Information	Remarks and references to Appendices
April 1st	Lieutenant A.H. Macgregor wounded. Captains H. Buchanan, G.E. Duncan to & Lieut S.L. Duncan taken over command of A, B, C and D Coys from Captain E.H. Clyne, Lieutenant H.A. Warington, Lieut ...., Captain ...... & C. R. Glover respectively.	Shelled & etc ... Capt J.H. Duncan Senior Capt ...
April 2nd	It was C and D Coys took over from A & B in INPUT VILLAGE. Platoon of the 9th Cavalry of London Reserve were attached to the Battalion for instructional purposes. Platoons of thirty ... were attached to the different Companies ... to the strength of ... This total strength now ... officers and 1140 other ranks. A count of ... Commanding ... not first ... ... held some time ... into the loss of ... ... Mountain ... ... at MECHELEN on November 1st. ... The ... given by R.S.G. that thirteen should be written off.	
April 3rd	It was a clouded ... with the BLACK WATCH to Cahyrnes. Headquarters the RUE DU BOIS Near CHOCOLAT MENIER corner. A Band C Coys with the twenty ... attached occupied the ...	

WAR DIARY

or

INTELLIGENCE SUMMARY

(Erase heading not required.)

Instructions regarding War Diaries and Intelligence
Summaries are contained in F. S. Regs, Part II.
and the Staff Manual respectively.   Title pages
will be prepared in manuscript.

Hour, Date, Place	Summary of Events and Information	Remarks and references to Appendices
April 6th	D Coy strained near Headquarters in Reserve.	
	An enemy mountain gun called "Pipsqueak" was much against us heart.	
	worked hard at their fill in the vicinity of the billets, but not doing any	
	damage. C Coy were relieved at night	
April 5th	21st Regiment was formed up into a unit and took over a portion of the	
	line, Major Richards being in Command. B Coy came out at night into the reserve.	
April 6th	Parapets strengthened and trenches drained and shelters behind	
	Posts to A, to B and to C completed. Barricade across gap north of HqDetachin	
	trenches about 3 bits. A Coy came out and 2 platoons of B	
	went in.	
April 7th	Right section of line. Parapets damaged by Shell fire repaired.	
	Centre section. 20 yards of parapet were rebuilt.	
	Left section. 150 sandbags built on left of parapet to complete	
	restoration of breach leading there from DEAD COW Farm.	
	At night changed back to reserve position at INDIAN VILLAGE.	
	A and B Coys went in and C and D Coys and the Jersey Coy remained in	
	Reserve.	
April 8th - 10th	Situation very quiet. Lieutenant H.C. Ghurka joined the Battalion	

WAR DIARY

or

INTELLIGENCE SUMMARY

(*Erase heading not required.*)

Instructions regarding War Diaries and Intelligence
Summaries are contained in F. S. Regs., Part II.
and the Staff Manual respectively. Title pages
will be prepared in manuscript.

Hour, Date, Place	Summary of Events and Information	Remarks and references to Appendices
April 10th	on list ? 3rd Regiment passed from under the command of the O.C. London Scottish In Afternoon a shell from a mountain gun killt wounding orea.	
April 11th	German aeroplanes were active for first time for many weeks flying several times over our lines. Again changed position with the BLACK WATCH. Plg. remained out ... D Company of the 232nd Regiment was attached by instructional purposes and was dealt with similarly to the 118th Regiment. It consisted of 6 Officers and 220 other Ranks. A shell fell in its billets, three wounding of of them.	
April 12th	A good deal of shelling on both sides. No casualties reported but two casualties	
April 13th	Officers of the WELSH Regiment who are to relieve us on the 15th shown over the defences. Also Machine Gun Officers of the ROYAL WELSH FUSILIERS who take over the Machine Gun Positions.	
April 15th	Relieved late at night. Battalion concentrated near LE TOURET	

1247 W 3299 200,000 (E) 8/14 J.B.C. & A. Forms/C. 2118/11.

Army Form C. 2118.

WAR DIARY
or
INTELLIGENCE SUMMARY
(Erase heading not required.)

Instructions regarding War Diaries and Intelligence Summaries are contained in F. S. Regs., Part II. and the Staff Manual respectively. Title pages will be prepared in manuscript.

Hour, Date, Place	Summary of Events and Information	Remarks and references to Appendices
April 17th	and marched to the Billets previously occupied by us at HINGETTE near BETHUNE: Arrived at 2.30 AM, April 16th. 48 Other Ranks transferred under Captain (?) (You are to not "Readier". Extract from London Gazette dated 15 April:— "16th London Regiment (London letter), Lieutenant to the temporary Captains to be temporary Captain H. L. Syer.— J. Paterson, H.B. Stribling (November 13)	
April 18th	Battalion in Brigade bathing from 6 P.M. 18th till 6 P.M. 19th.	
April 19–20th	Battalion in rest at HINGETTE	
April 23rd	Battalion moved to ALOUAGNE	
April 24–25th	Company Training	
April 26th	Battalion training for the attack in the wood	
April 27th	Company training	LE MAREQUET.
April 28th	Battalion training in the wood LE MAREQUET.	
April 30th	Battalion training in the Bois DES DAMES	

1247 W 3299 200,000 (E) 8/14 J.B.C. & A.   Forms/C. 2118/11.

1st Infantry Brigade.

1st Division.

WAR
DIARY

LONDON   SCOTTISH

(14th London Regiment)

M   A   Y

1 9 1 5

1 Map.

WAR DIARY

or

INTELLIGENCE SUMMARY

(Erase heading not required.)

Instructions regarding War Diaries and Intelligence Summaries are contained in F. S. Regs., Part II. and the Staff Manual respectively. Title pages will be prepared in manuscript.

Hour, Date, Place		Summary of Events and Information	Remarks and references to Appendices
May		LONDON SCOTTISH. 14 RN LONDON RT	
	1.	Preparations to move.	
	2.	Battalion marched to Reserve Billets at RICHEBOURG St MART	
		and is in Brigade Reserve	
	3.	Battalion moved at night to support works about 300ᵗ	
	4.	N. of RUE DU BOIS	
	5.	1 Corporal killed	
	6.		
	7.		
	8.	Battalion received orders to move into a position	
		presently at RICHEBOURG St MART preparatory to an attack on	
		the German positions south of R. CHEBOURG L'AVOUE the 2 and	
	3ʳᵈ	Brigades finding the firing line and supports and the	
		1st Brigade being in reserve.	
	9.	Bombardment of enemy's line began at 5-0 A.M.	
		and assault at 5-40 A.M. When the assaulting battalions	

1247 W 3399 200,000 (E) 8/14 J.B.C. & A.   Forms/C. 2118/11.

WAR DIARY

or

INTELLIGENCE SUMMARY — LONDON SCOTTISH (14th BN. LONDON REGT)

(Erase heading not required.)

Instructions regarding War Diaries and Intelligence Summaries are contained in F. S. Regs., Part II. and the Staff Manual respectively. Title pages will be prepared in manuscript.

Hour, Date, Place	Summary of Events and Information	Remarks and references to Appendices
	had left these lines. The battalion at 6-7 A.M. commenced to move across the open ground to occupy a entrenchment near to RUE DU BOIS. The enemy having failed to receive a footing in the enemy's lines, it was delivered again after a similar bombardment at 4 P.M. The 4th & 6th (The Black Watch) and the Cameron Highlanders checked and the Germans carried the First line of trenches and reached the second. This Battalion was kept in close support in case of a Counterattack by the Enemy. The men of the 42nd who had gained the position were nearly all killed or wounded and thus the First Brigade was relieved by units of the 2nd Division and this Battalion marched into billets at HINGES. Casualties. 10 Officers 3 Other Ranks killed, 35 other Ranks wounded. The following messages were received :—	

Army Form C. 2118.

WAR DIARY
or
INTELLIGENCE SUMMARY

(Erase heading not required.)

LONDON SCOTTISH (14ᵗʰ Bⁿ LONDᵒⁿ Rᵗ)

Instructions regarding War Diaries and Intelligence
Summaries are contained in F. S. Regs., Part II.
and the Staff Manual respectively. Title pages
will be prepared in manuscript.

Hour, Date, Place	Summary of Events and Information	Remarks and references to Appendices
	The General Officer Commanding 1st Guard. Brigade.	

The General Officers
Commanding 1st Army, and the General Officers Commanding &
wish to express to the officers non-commissioned officers
and men of the 1st Guard. Brigade their deep appreciation
of the efforts of attempts to carry by assault the enemy's
defences in front of the R.V.E. du Bois on the 9th May.

On my own behalf I shall be glad if you will tell the
Commanding Officers to inform their Battalions that nothing
could have exceeded the gallantry displayed by officers &
other ranks in the assault.

I deeply regret the casualties which occurred but
they were not in vain. By their example and example should
rest of us a fine example of how such an assault should
be delivered. From a military point of view the attack was
of the greatest value because it was very hostile reinforcements urgently required to repel the successful attack

45

LONDON Scottish (14ᵗʰ Bⁿ LONDᵒⁿ Rᵗ)

Army Form C. 2118.

Instructions regarding War Diaries and Intelligence
Summaries are contained in F. S. Regs., Part II.
and the Staff Manual respectively. Title pages
will be prepared in manuscript.

WAR DIARY
or
INTELLIGENCE SUMMARY

(Erase heading not required.)

LONDON SCOTTISH (14th Bn LONDON RT)

Hour, Date, Place	Summary of Events and Information	Remarks and references to Appendices
	attack to the south. These statements coming up towards our front formed an excellent target for our heavy Guns, who fired on them both, great effect. Aeroplane reconnaissance also reports heavy Casualties in the enemy's lines just in rear of his breastwork. We are observed state that these casualties alone exceed those of our men on both sides of his breastworks. Irish I wish also to convey to the officers Commanding the Division by the successful assault of part of his leading lines, a feat of arms which the battalion must always be proud of as this Battalion was the only one in the Brigade whose been succeeded in storming the enemy's breastworks.	

1st Division HQ.
11th May, 1915.

Major General
Commanding 1st Division

1247 W 3299 200,000 (E) 8/14 J.B.C. &A.   Forms/C. 2118/11.

Army Form C. 2118.

WAR DIARY
or
INTELLIGENCE SUMMARY

(Erase heading not required.)

Instructions regarding War Diaries and Intelligence Summaries are contained in F. S. Regs., Part II. and the Staff Manual respectively. Title pages will be prepared in manuscript.

(14 BN LONDON R?)

LONDON SCOTTISH

Hour, Date, Place	Summary of Events and Information	Remarks and references to Appendices

Headquarters,
1st Army
10th Mar 1915.

Special Order.

The following message received from G.O.C. 1st Army from the Field Marshal, Commander-in-Chief, established for information and communication to the troops, invites Corps Command :—

"In reviewing to you and the troops of the First Army my warm appreciation of ???? work yesterday, I wish to have known to you that, in addition, to the lateral success gained by the 8th Division in Capturing and holding the enemy's trenches at ???? important point the attacks made all along our line proved of great assurance to our gallant allies on the right. All the British Army will rejoice to hear that the French 10th Army between our right and ARRAS drove the enemy back all along the front and at one point advanced as much as 5—

1247 W 3299 200,000 (E) 8/14 J.B.C. & A. Forms/C. 2118/11.

WAR DIARY

INTELLIGENCE SUMMARY

(Erase heading not required.)

LONDON SCOTTISH (14th BN LONDON RT)

Instructions regarding War Diaries and Intelligence Summaries are contained in F. S. Regs., Part II. and the Staff Manual respectively. Title pages will be prepared in manuscript.

Hour, Date, Place	Summary of Events and Information	Remarks and references to Appendices
	kilometres. In addition our allies captured 8 field guns, 2 heavy guns, many machine guns, and about 12,000 prisoners. (Signed) R. Butler, Brigadier-General, General Staff, 1st Army.	
10th	In billets at HINGES.	
11th	Battalion was on duty, inhabitants being in triple reserve.	
12th	9PM – Battalion marched to GIVENCHY and took over the FRENCH BRITISH-FRENCH sector from the 3rd GRENADIER GUARDS, the trenches being the first that the Battalion has ever taken over.	
13th	Battalion relieved by 19th County of London Regiment and marched to Billet North of BETHUNE. The last Company arriving at 5AM.	
14th	Orders were received that the 1st Division should take over a portion of the line South of LA BASSEE-BETHUNE road from the French. Battalion took over about and left a rest of the trenches East of VERMELLES. Relieving 11 Coy of the 290th and D Coy of the 296th Regiment. A 1/2 Batt. of Battalion left near VERMELLES from which communication trenches led to left. A Coy relieved 6 Coy and Bloc held D. 2 Platoons of 6 Coy were left in the trenches English relief lines.	
15th		
17th		

1247 W 3299 200,000 (E) 8/14 J.B.C. & A. Forms/C. 2118/11.

LONDON SCOTTISH

Army Form C. 2118.

WAR DIARY
and
INTELLIGENCE SUMMARY

(Erase heading not required.)

Instructions regarding War Diaries and Intelligence
Summaries are contained in F.S. Regs., Part II.
and the Staff Manual respectively. Title pages
will be prepared in manuscript.

Hour, Date, Place	Summary of Events and Information	Remarks and references to Appendices
	LONDON SCOTTISH.	
May 16th.	Captain James H Lindsay joined the Battalion this day, having been promoted to 2/O Battalion	
May 17th.		
" 18th	Rations are now carried to the Trenches on Pack Animals, Bridges having been put over C.T. for that purpose.	(reference attached) Sketch. dated 19.5.15
" 19th	Chief work from now onwards is rendering C.T. 53 practicable.	
" 20th	Craters to enable water to be carried on Pack Animals made — Water carried up at night.	
" 21st.		
" 22nd		
" 23rd	Work of connecting across two salients in trenches begun by boring and digging a new Trench behind here.	

signed Alexander
Capt A.A.S.W.
LONDON SCOTTISH

1247 W 8299 200,000 (E) 8/14 J.B.C. & A. Forms/C. 2118/11.

LONDON SCOTTISH

WAR DIARY

INTELLIGENCE SUMMARY

(Erase heading not required.)

Instructions regarding War Diaries and Intelligence
Summaries are contained in F. S. Regs., Part II.
and the Staff Manual respectively. Title pages
will be prepared in manuscript.

Hour, Date, Place	Summary of Events and Information LONDON SCOTTISH	Remarks and references to Appendices
May 24th	Machine Gun emplacement to traverse front of wire begun.	
May 25th		
" 26th	Details of a Point d'Appui and C.T. 53 discussed. to be made round ruined House. C.T. 8 to be held by a small Sub post near P. A. 20 & flocked with that of emerging arm.	
" 27th		
" 28th	Machine Gun position about 200 Y behind trenches begun as a supporting point in C.T. 53	
" 29th		
" 30th		
" 31st	Battalion received orders that it will be relieved to-morrow night by the 8th Battalion London Regiment.	

(signature)
Capt. Adjutant
LONDON SCOTTISH

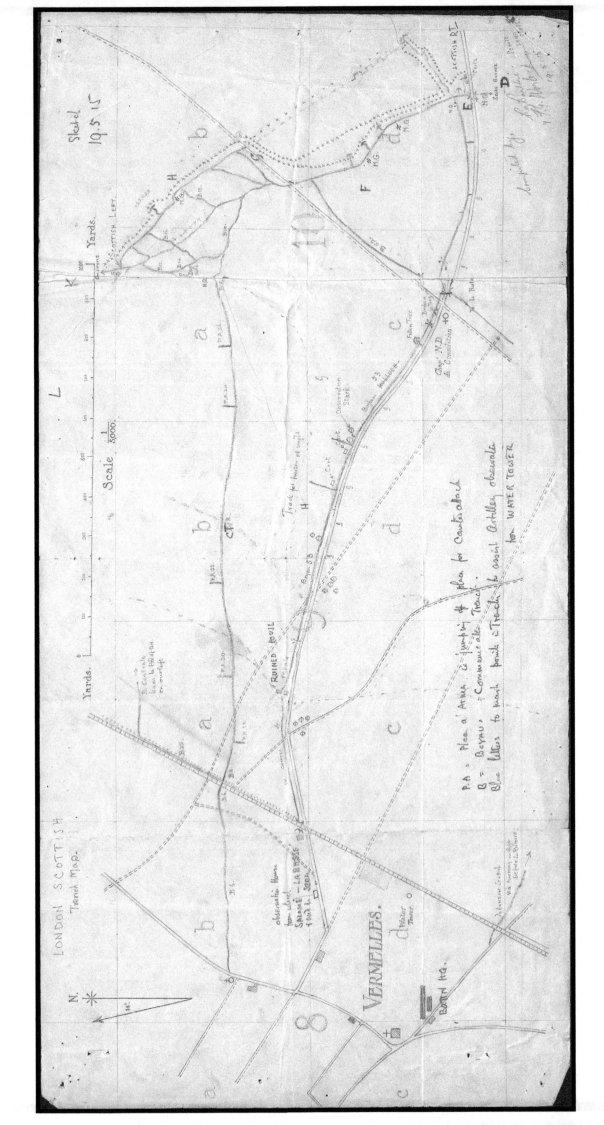

WAR
DIARY

L O N D O N   S C O T T I S H

(14th London Regiment)

J U N E

1 9 1 5

2 Maps.

Army Form C. 2118.

WAR DIARY
or
INTELLIGENCE SUMMARY.
(Erase heading not required.)

Instructions regarding War Diaries and Intelligence Summaries are contained in F. S. Regs., Part II. and the Staff Manual respectively. Title pages will be prepared in manuscript.

LONDON SCOTTISH.

June.

Hour, Date, Place	Summary of Events and Information	Remarks and references to Appendices
VERMELLES June 1st	General ARENBERG of M.V.O. of the Danish Army visited the Battalion in the Trenches. He congratulated on the reputation it had won on service.	
	Battalion was relieved by the 8th London Battalion (Post Office Rifles) and moved into Billets at BETHUNE.	
BETHUNE " 2nd	Orders were received that no issue of leave in future after this date.	
" 3rd	In Billets and cleaning up.	
" 4th	The Battalion went to Summer Baths.	
" 5th	The Battalion had letters assessed by the R.A.M.C.	
" 6th		
" 7th	In billets. Companies went Route March and to Summer Baths.	
	Battalion was inspected by Lieut General Sir Charles Munro K.C.B. Commanding 1st Corps who expressed himself as very pleased with the appearance of the Battalion on parade.	

Lennox Allison
Capt O.A.S/r.

(9 20 6) W 2794 100,000 8/14 H W V   Forms/C. 2118/11.

LONDON SCOTTISH

WAR DIARY

or

INTELLIGENCE SUMMARY.

(Erase heading not required.)

Instructions regarding War Diaries and Intelligence Summaries are contained in F.S. Regs., Part II. and the Staff Manual respectively. Title pages will be prepared in manuscript.

Hour, Date, Place	Summary of Events and Information	Remarks and references to Appendices
BETHUNE June 8th.	Battalion move to Reserve Billets at ANNEQUIN, the Brigade	
" 9th.	holding the Sector from the Railway Embankment near CUINCHY to about 500 yards south of the BETHUNE — LA BASSEE road.	
" 10th.	N° 213 Sergeant N. McGregor Gow, N°717 Corporal S. I. Stott and N°1607 Lance Corporal D. A. Stewart were notified that they had been awarded the D.C.M.	
	N° 213 Sergeant N McGregor Gow behaved with coolness on 31st October near MESSINES and during the attack on GIVENCHY in the latter part of December. Particularly in Connection with reconnaissance of the gap between the 1st and 3rd Brigades. He has behaved in an exceptionally brave manner under fire throughout the campaign.	
	N° 717 Corporal S. I. Stott behaved with great gallantry at YPRES when the Battalion was in the trenches near	

James Gillan
Capt OR O S.

WAR DIARY

or

INTELLIGENCE SUMMARY.

(Erase heading not required.)

LONDON SCOTTISH

Instructions regarding War Diaries and Intelligence Summaries are contained in F. S. Regs., Part II. and the Staff Manual respectively. Title pages will be prepared in manuscript.

Hour, Date, Place	Summary of Events and Information	Remarks and references to Appendices
	KIEN ZILLEBEKE and has done good work throughout the campaign. No 1607 Lance corporal D.A. Stewart behaved with gallantry at MESSINES on October 31st and on many subsequent occasions. His behaviour has been exemplary at all times and under all circumstances throughout the campaign.	
ANNEQUIN. July 16th	During the last 3 weeks a very large number of obliterating.	
	No Commissions from the ranks have been recommended by the Commanding Officer resulting in the loss to the Battalion of a large number of its best men.	
" 17th	Each day while in reserve the Battalion has supplied (to the allied) fatigue working parties which have been found by mining the trade.	
	The General Brigade and Battalion Orders specially board Officers and NC Men who were named	
	"the subject of bombing is not sufficiently seriously considered in all Battalions of this Brigade, tactics both above & below & ground are an unimportant accessory in fighting.	

(9 29 6) W 2794 100,000 8/14 H W V   Forms/C. 2118/11.

Lancaster
Capt LNSA

WAR DIARY

or

INTELLIGENCE SUMMARY.

(Erase heading not required.)

Instructions regarding War Diaries and Intelligence Summaries are contained in F. S. Regs., Part II. and the Staff Manual respectively. Title pages will be prepared in manuscript.

Hour, Date, Place	Summary of Events and Information	Remarks and references to Appendices
	This is chiefly because the Bn. while has never happened to be confronted with a situation where the want of such has been essential. From the accounts given by Officers who have taken part in the operations between Givenchy and Rue du Bois it is very evident that the use of bombs is becoming both to extend a partial success & gained by to extend attack and to confirm any advantage achieved.	
	In our Bn. the ideas and efforts being made to train every man in the use of bombs; the advance to the point of view of those who have been engaged in bomb fights. It is felt in my opinion necessary to try to extend training to that extent that a sufficient reserve of trained men must always be available to maintain a sufficient supply of bombers. Every Battalion is to have a Battalion Bomb Officer, the duty will be far more important than those of a Platoon Commander, as	

Army Form C. 2118.

WAR DIARY
or
INTELLIGENCE SUMMARY

(Erase heading not required.)

Instructions regarding War Diaries and Intelligence Summaries are contained in F. S. Regs., Part II. and the Staff Manual respectively. Title pages will be prepared in manuscript.

Hour, Date, Place	Summary of Events and Information	Remarks and references to Appendices
	Shortage of officers will not be accepted as a reason for no such officer being detailed.	
	His duties will be, under the direction of the C.O., to maintain a supply of men trained in bombing up to 100 head (with a proportion of N.C.O's) per Battalion.	
	He will be responsible in defence for the locating of bomb parties, for their relief and for the requisite bomb stores and their position, and will see that every man knows his duty in case any part of our trenches is rushed.	
	In attack he will assist in the organisation of bomb parties, in close collaboration with the Coy. Commanders and will be responsible for the bringing forward of the reserve supply of bombs. (The latter is probably his most important duty.)	
	The use of a great number of live bombs in training is not necessary use; for the rest that training men largely be carried out with dummy bombs. Whenever officers obtain confidence in the weapons they have to use; for the rest that training men largely be carried out with dummy bombs.	
	Commanding Officers will see that the provisions of this order are carried into effect.	
	(Signed) A. C. Lowther	
	Brig. General	
	Commanding 1st Guards Bde.	
	H.Q. 1st Guards Bde. 9th June, 1915	
	The following are the Battalion Orders dated 12/6/15:	

1247 W 8299 200,000 (E) 8/14 J.B.C. & A. Forms/C. 2118/11.

Army Form C. 2118.

LAWTON SCOTT

WAR DIARY
INTELLIGENCE SUMMARY

(Erase heading not required.)

Instructions regarding War Diaries and Intelligence Summaries are contained in F. S. Regs., Part II. and the Staff Manual respectively. Title pages will be prepared in manuscript.

Hour, Date, Place	Summary of Events and Information	Remarks and references to Appendices
	Battalion Bomb and Grenade Throwers	

1. Lieut J.C. Brown-Constable is appointed Battalion Bomb Officer
   (Battalion Orders No 191, Para 3 dated 11/6/15)

2. There will be one N.C.O. and 12 Bombers in each Coy. One of these
   N.C.O.'s will be a sergeant.
   The Bomb officer will ascertain the number of other
   men and of 25 men in each Coy. have been trained.

3. When the C.O. considers it desirable that a particular task
   should be allotted to the Battalion Bombers, such numbers
   he directs will be selected by the Bomb Officer again will be detailed
   from these Coys. under the orders of the Bomb officer.
   C.O. bombs will be was Throwable, use bombers as such
   and not as rifle Co.
   When the Battalion is in the Trenches the Bomb officer will
   advise the C.O. as to the number of men he considers it
   would be suitable to post as Bomb Parties and as to the points
   in which he considers they would be well placed. The number will
   include reliefs. Parties detailed will be posted by the Bomb
   Officer. He is responsible for their relief and the adequate
   Bomb stores and he will see that every Officer and N.C.O. is acquainted
   his position and his duty in case any part of our trenches

1247   W 3299   200,000   (E)   8/14   J.B.C. & A.   Forms/C. 2118/11.

WAR DIARY

or

INTELLIGENCE SUMMARY

(Erase heading not required.)

Army Form C. 2118.

LONDON SCOTTISH

Instructions regarding War Diaries and Intelligence
Summaries are contained in F. S. Regs., Part II.
and the Staff Manual respectively.   Title pages
will be prepared in manuscript.

Hour, Date, Place	Summary of Events and Information	Remarks and references to Appendices

is finished.

4. In attack the Bomb Officer will assist in the organisation of Bomb Parties in collaboration with Company Commanders. He will be responsible for keeping forward reserve supplies of Bombs.

(sd.) James Paterson
Capt. & Adjutant.

CAMBRIN, June 13th.

Battalion relieved the 1st CAMERON HIGHLANDERS in the Section South of the LA BASSEE Road of which two sketch maps are attached. It will be noted that this is part of the ground recently taken over by the British from the French.

The peculiarities of the ground here are those of a recent mining and counter-mining), that have given between them, resulting in huge craters in the ground intervening possession of which is struggled for by each side, infested by the rifle — and hand grenades thrown by the other.

The C.O. has under his Command the Coy. of GUARDS near his Battalion Headquarters which are situated on the reverse slope of the hill about 500x E. of CAMBRIN Church in a dug-out constructed

Vivian Pater
Capt

WAR DIARY

or

INTELLIGENCE SUMMARY

(Erase heading not required.)

Instructions regarding War Diaries and Intelligence
Summaries are contained in F. S. Regs, Part II.
and the Staff Manual respectively.   Title pages
will be prepared in manuscript.

LONDONS 6TTM

Hour, Date, Place	Summary of Events and Information	Remarks and references to Appendices
	of semi-circular boiler plates built into the ground these but against front complete protection against heavy shell fire that this battalion has yet seen.	
June 14th	An enemy bomb following trenches to throw scattering. It is a hand grenade, about the size of a 1 lb. jam Tin very well made, with a wooden handle about 9" long with a side of the middle of it. It is strongly carefully designed and well made. The grenade is now supplied with is known as BETHUNE bomb and is composed of a cast-iron cylinder 3" long and 2" in diameter, a circular ring of gun- cotton inside detonated in the usual way. ignition of the fuse being by winding down a cord. howitzer tube Wheel over the fuse wire, which generates a spark igniting the fuse. It will thus be seen that this is not a very safe weapon and is have had identified.	

WAR DIARY

or

INTELLIGENCE SUMMARY

(Erase heading not required.)

Instructions regarding War Diaries and Intelligence Summaries are contained in F. S. Regs., Part II. and the Staff Manual respectively. Title pages will be prepared in manuscript.

Hour, Date, Place	Summary of Events and Information	Remarks and references to Appendices
June 15th.	1 wounded through premature explosion to-day. Yesterday afternoon it became evident that the Germans were taking possession of the mine craters opposite us. Arrangements were therefore made through the 1st GUARDS BDE. to clear all our first line of trenches opposite this place, while the 60th Howitzer Battery and 115th R.F.A. opened fire at the German Trenches and the craters. The result was greatly diminished activity on the part of the Germans. Another death and another wounded through premature explosion of bomb.	
June 16th.	The whole of the Battalion is now issued with 61th Helmets and bellards London Constabulary to cover the head and tuck in under the coat in case of a Gas attack, the respirators formerly issued being retained in case the Helmet to bear became ineffective. The bombardment of yesterday was repeated with the same precautions. The following Battalion After Orders here fulfilled. Reference 1st Division 2021. Battalion Orders No 162, Para I of 11th May.
\
\
Wounded. 1. The task of giving first aid to wounded and of placing	

Army Form C. 2118.

LONDON SCOTTISH.

WAR DIARY

~~INTELLIGENCE SUMMARY~~

(Erase heading not required.)

Instructions regarding War Diaries and Intelligence Summaries are contained in F. S. Regs., Part II. and the Staff Manual respectively. Title pages will be prepared in manuscript.

Hour, Date, Place	Summary of Events and Information	Remarks and references to Appendices
	them in a place of Comparative safety during an action (if thou be in the Battalion Aid Post) (a) In the present warfare where movement forward is extended & small and where fighting continues on the same front for several days, the normal number of stretcher bearers is not enough. (b) The above that therefore devolves on the actual firing line engaged. The method of doing this will be by certain men being told off by Company Commanders before and during an action. (Vide B^n Orders, N° 162, Para (1) dated 11/5/15. 2. The task of clearing these men back to the dressing station, if they are not already got there by dark, will be done by the regimental stretcher bearers, assisted by men specially detailed before an action commences, such as Pioneers & the normal bearers of such men may have to be filled by men fit for light duty only. stretchers for both these classes of special bearers can be obtained through the Medical Officer as soon as he knows that an action is imminent. Companies who establish "places of Comparative safety" other than the Battalion Aid Post must provide guides	

1247   W 3299   200,000   (E)   8/14   J.B.C. & A.   Forms/C. 2118/11.

Lauren Allen
Capt

WAR DIARY
or
INTELLIGENCE SUMMARY.
(*Erase heading not required.*)

Instructions regarding War Diaries and Intelligence
Summaries are contained in F. S. Regs., Part II.
and the Staff Manual respectively. Title pages
will be prepared in manuscript.

Hour, Date, Place	Summary of Events and Information	Remarks and references to Appendices
CAMBRIN-BETHUNE. June 17th	three days is to see to their organization. Officers who detail them to help wounded should if it should give them are not so that they cannot be accused of shirking their duty in the fight. (sigd) James Lister, Major.	
BETHUNE. June 18th	BETHUNE. Battalion was relieved by 2nd King's Royal Rifles. Relief was rather difficult owing to shell fire. Battalion moved into billets at BETHUNE.	
BETHUNE.	Battalion was on duty on short notice, being in Corps Reserve. Men were needed to the Winning Baths in the afternoon and to the Hot Baths in the afternoon. The following Battalion Order was Published:- "The Commanding Officer congratulates the Battalion on the excellent work it had done during the past three days under difficult and novel conditions. "The energy and persistency with which all ranks behaved, changed the totality of the head into an attitude of anticipation."	
BETHUNE - LAPUGNOY. June 19th June 20th	Moved to Billets at LAPUGNOY. Church Parade.	

James Lister
Captain Adjt.

1247 W 3299 200,000 (E) 8/14 J.B.C. & A. Forms/C. 2118/11.

WAR DIARY

or

INTELLIGENCE SUMMARY

(Erase heading not required.)

Instructions regarding War Diaries and Intelligence
Summaries are contained in F. S. Regs., Part II.
and the Staff Manual respectively. Title pages
will be prepared in manuscript.

Hour, Date, Place	Summary of Events and Information	Remarks and references to Appendices
LAVIGNOY. 21st June	Battalion Practised the attack in the Bois per Daniel against an Enemy Composed of Battalion Scouts Machine Gun Section and other specialists. Attempts by the latter to gain information through representing peasants were frustrated; a large number of the Battalion was successfully ambushed.	
LAVIGNOY. 22nd June.	A large number of N.C.O's and men are still being Recommended for Commissions. Company Training. Attack with bomb and bayonet was practised.	
23rd June		

WAR DIARY

or

INTELLIGENCE SUMMARY

(Erase heading not required.)

Instructions regarding War Diaries and Intelligence Summaries are contained in F. S. Regs., Part II. and the Staff Manual respectively. Title pages will be prepared in manuscript.

Hour, Date, Place	Summary of Events and Information	Remarks and references to Appendices
(AUG.NO?)- HURIONVILLE. June 24th.	Battalion marched to Billets at HURIONVILLE. The following are mentioned in Dispatches relating to the period previous to the Despatch of April 5th 1915, published May 31st — Lieut Colonel B.C. Green. T.D. Captain C.H. Campbell. "CAMERON HIGHLANDERS" (Adjutant) Lieutenant J. Paterson. Lieutenant (Temporary Captain) H.C. Stellary. " " 4th N.Scottyton. Lieutenant (now Temp. Captain) D. Lyall Grant. Lieutenant (" ") D. J. Chisholm. No. 1753. Lance Corporal Company Training.	
HURIONVILLE. June 25th		

[signature]
Capt R A?

Army Form C. 2118.

WAR DIARY
or
INTELLIGENCE SUMMARY
(Erase heading not required.)

Instructions regarding War Diaries and Intelligence Summaries are contained in F. S. Regs., Part II. and the Staff Manual respectively. Title pages will be prepared in manuscript.

LONDON SCOTTISH.

Hour, Date, Place	Summary of Events and Information	Remarks and references to Appendices
HURIONVILLE. June 26th	Company and Musketry Training. The following is an extract from Battalion Orders of this date:- H.M. The King has been graciously pleased to give the directions for the following appointments. To be a Companion of the Most Distinguished Order of St. Michael and St. George. Lieut. Colonel B.G. Green, T.D. To be a Companion of the Distinguished Service Order. Captain C.H. Campbell. CAMERON HIGHLANDERS (attached LONDON SCOTTISH) Awarded the Military Cross. Lieutenant (Tidway Captain) James Paterson. Lieutenant 27.1621 R.A.M.C. (attached LONDON SCOTTISH)	
HURIONVILLE. June 27th June 28th	Church Parade and Musketry Training. Company Training.	
HURIONVILLE–FOUQUEREUIL June 29th FOUQUEREUIL. June 30th	Battalion moved to Billets at FOUQUEREUIL. Company and Musketry Training.	

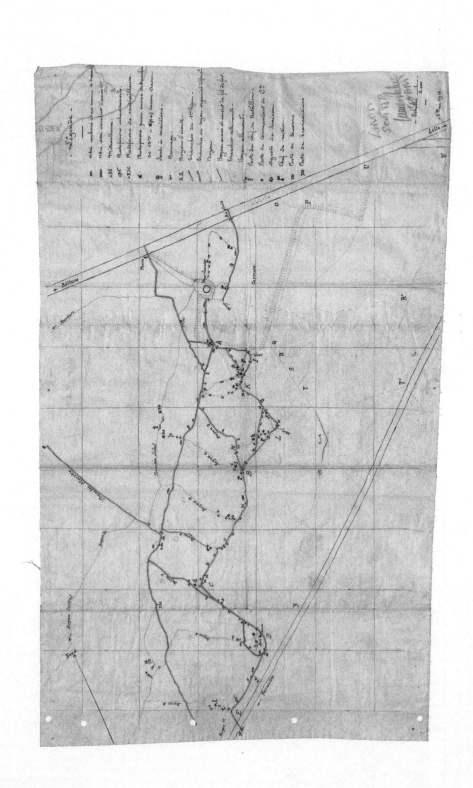

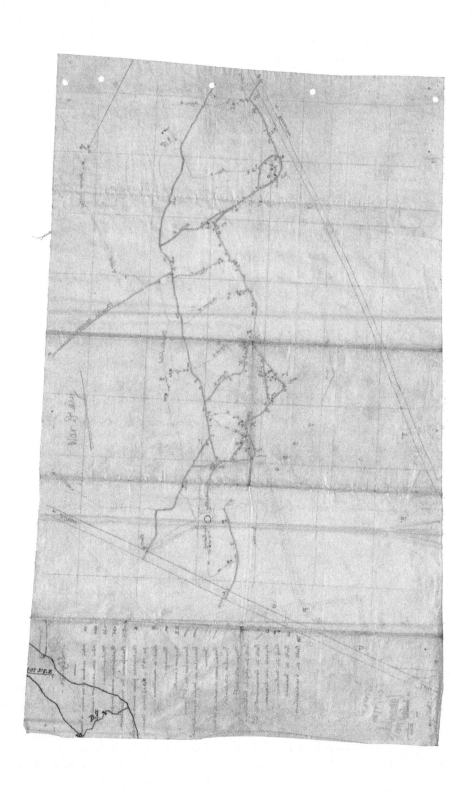

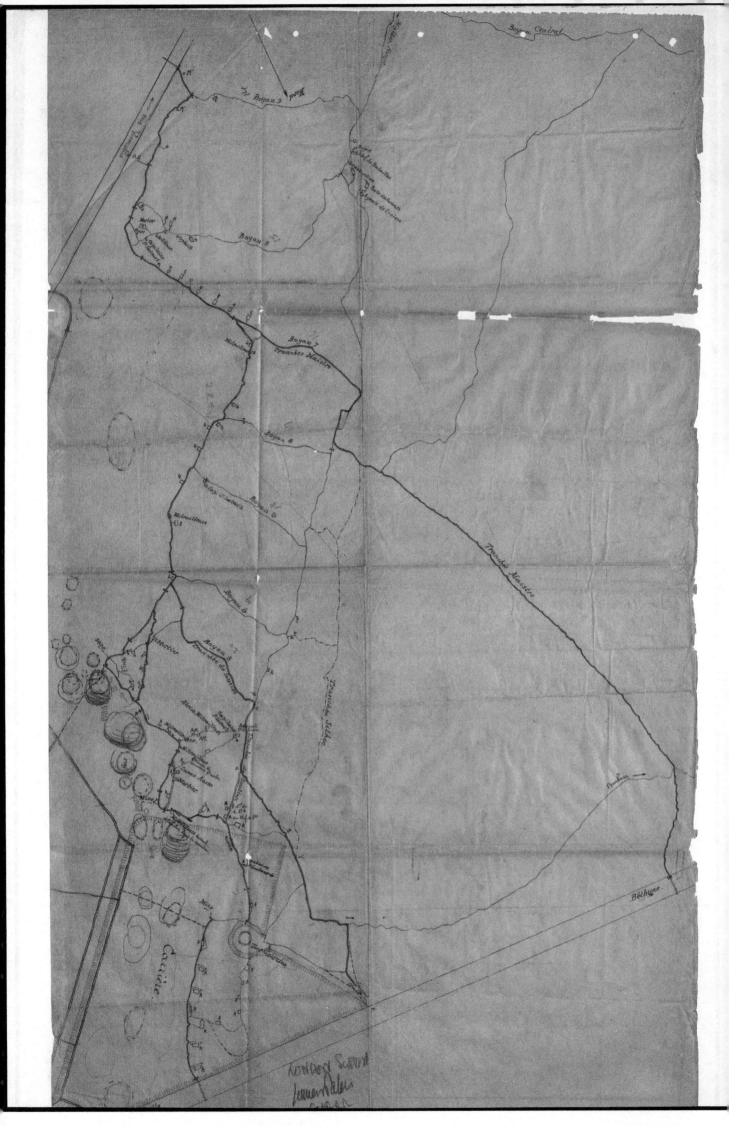

WAR
DIARY

LONDON   SCOTTISH

(14th London Regiment)

J U L Y

1 9 1 5

WAR DIARY
of
INTELLIGENCE SUMMARY

LONDON SCOTTISH.

(Erase heading not required.)

Instructions regarding War Diaries and Intelligence Summaries are contained in F. S. Regs., Part II. and the Staff Manual respectively. Title pages will be prepared in manuscript.

Hour, Date, Place	Summary of Events and Information	Remarks and references to Appendices
1915. July 1. FOUQUEREUIL	Company and Musketry training, and instruction in First Aid.	
2.	Practice of attack on Trenches with Bombers and Bayonet.	
3.	Company training.	
4.	Company training.	
5.	Church Parade.	
	Battalion moved to Support Billets in the village of VERMELLES. arriving about 11 p.m., the Brigade occupying a front of 2 Battalions the two sections on the right and left of the Canal Bassée to la Bassée station between VERMELLES and HULLOCH.	
6. VERMELLES.	The Chapel of Notre Dame la	
7. 8. 9. 10. 11.	Battalion formed a large number of Working Parties engaged in Keeps and dug outs and in strengthening the line.	
	During the last few days arrangements have been made	

Cavendish
Capt. A.O.C.

2.

Army Form C. 2118.

LHDO11 &975/94.

WAR DIARY
or
INTELLIGENCE SUMMARY
(Erase heading not required.)

Instructions regarding War Diaries and Intelligence Summaries are contained in F. S. Regs., Part II. and the Staff Manual respectively. Title pages will be prepared in manuscript.

Hour, Date, Place	Summary of Events and Information	Remarks and references to Appendices
July 12.	For all ranks have been out with the Battalion since the beginning of the War to get leave time in turn. This absence fourteen per week have been arranged for. This is very grateful appreciated. A very large number of men continue to leave in turn to take commissions. The Battalion took over the sector of trenches immediately in front of the CHAPELLE de NOTRE DAME at CONSERVATION, two Companies being in the front line. The trenches have been much improved since the Battalion first took over the line by connecting up the various considerably disturbed to ... when A Company built a Sapping line have constructed about 300 yards of the firing line which owns a great improvement. The Battalion has received a gift of two Baths and a telling apparatus which was established in a Bath House by the Sappers company at VERMELLES, and it is proposed to establish similar institutions elsewhere be we	

1247 W 3290 200,000 (E) 8/14 J.B.C. & A. Forms/C. 2118/11.

[signature] Captain

Army Form C. 2118.

WAR DIARY
or
INTELLIGENCE SUMMARY

(Erase heading not required.)

10th Batt SCOTTISH

Instructions regarding War Diaries and Intelligence
Summaries are contained in F.S. Regs., Part II.
and the Staff Manual respectively. Title pages
will be prepared in manuscript.

Hour, Date, Place	Summary of Events and Information	Remarks and references to Appendices
July 13.	In the Trenches.	
16.	Lieutenants Duncan, Macgregor and Gardiner joined the Battalion this day. The Brigade having relieved the appointment of one officer to perform the time attachment in front of the whole Brigade, Lieut Mr Sparks was selected 10th Brigade. Lieut him out below other Ranks Sergeant Bunn to various him and other Battalions in the Brigade, from each of the other Battalions. Captain J. Patison was appointed Adjutant from the 2nd Argyll & Suth (List No 37 of Appointments to Commissions. Rewards etc appeared by the Field Marshal Commanding in Chief, the Force in the Field, dated 10th July 1915).	
18.	G.O.C. 1st Division expressed his great admiration of the way in which the Battalion cleaned and maintained the village of VERMELLES.	
19.	The Battalion was relieved by the 5th ROYAL SUSSEX Regiment and moved to the Orphanage, BETHUNE.	

247 W 3299 200,000 (E) 8/14 J.B.C. & A.   Forms/C. 2118/11.

Army Form C. 2118.

WAR DIARY
or
INTELLIGENCE SUMMARY
(Erase heading not required.)

LONDON. 15027/194.

Instructions regarding War Diaries and Intelligence Summaries are contained in F. S. Regs., Part II. and the Staff Manual respectively. Title pages will be prepared in manuscript.

Hour, Date, Place	Summary of Events and Information	Remarks and references to Appendices
BETHUNE. Feb. 20.	The period on the whole has been very quiet. A generally moved away to the way breaking over ground instead of through a communication trench, at a distance of 1200 yards from the germans who fired several "pit spurts." several metres of communicating trench took place in the long grass between the lines.	
21.	The Brigadier General expressed his satisfaction with the amount of work carried out by the 2 hundls Brigade last out to the trenches.	
22. 23.	The Battalion went into Rue de Marais Barbing and Musketry practice was carried out and it has been averaged. Ditto. Ditto. Smoke helmets have now been issued to all men, these of plain cloth impregnated with some solution, with a window made of celluloid. They appear to be a	

Army Form C. 2118.

WAR DIARY

or

INTELLIGENCE SUMMARY

LONDON SCOTTISH

(Erase heading not required.)

Instructions regarding War Diaries and Intelligence Summaries are contained in F. S. Regs., Part II. and the Staff Manual respectively. Title pages will be prepared in manuscript.

Hour, Date, Place	Summary of Events and Information	Remarks and references to Appendices
Feb. 24.	Well-conducted attack. Difficulty however is experienced in hurrying the attack from crossing. 1st French Brigade seen in a force close near ANNEZIN Start was very well attended, and the trials of the Regimental Boxing Match of the Battalion made two ties.	
25.	Battalion moves to CAMBRIN and form groups for from Keeps situated between the BETHUNE – LA BASSÉE Road and the VERMELLES – LA BASSÉE Railway – about 35 men in each. The Keeps are to contain all things necessary for a 3 days' fight. The remaining two of four B Companies are in the MAISON ROUGE supporting line about 1000 yards E. of CAMBRIN CHURCH, C Company being in Dug Outs S. of the Church, and D Company at the sabeine broken end of the village.	

Capt A D O

Army Form C. 2118.

WAR DIARY
INTELLIGENCE SUMMARY
(Erase heading not required.)

Instructions regarding War Diaries and Intelligence Summaries are contained in F. S. Regs., Part II. and the Staff Manual respectively. Title pages will be prepared in manuscript.

LONDON SCOTTISH

Hour, Date, Place	Summary of Events and Information	Remarks and references to Appendices
26. CAMBRIN 29. 30. 31.	The work done by the Battalion during the past few days has been the completion of the keeps in order to conduct the entrance to such a way as to enable the keeps to be kept at least 30 yards away. The construction of a fire trench along the crest of the Hill F. of MAISON ROUGE, and the completion of splinter proof shelter to and the CAMBRIN CHURCH and D Company Billets in CAMBRIN, and the having of a Communication Trench from there to MAISON ROUGE. Fatigue parties have been supplied to the R.E. to the Brigade, firing and Bomb Officers and for establishing a Bomb store for S.A.A. and Bombs. There being no good map of the position of Trenches one has been made by the Scouts of ...

1247 W 3299 200,000 (E) 8/14 J.B.C. & A. Forms/C. 2118/11.

WAR
DIARY

LONDON SCOTTISH

(14th London Regiment)

A U G U S T

1 9 1 5

3 Diagrams.
1 Map.

Army Form C. 2118.

WAR DIARY
or
INTELLIGENCE SUMMARY
(Erase heading not required.)

LONDON SCOTTISH

Instructions regarding War Diaries and Intelligence Summaries are contained in F. S. Regs., Part II. and the Staff Manual respectively. Title pages will be prepared in manuscript.

Hour, Date, Place	Summary of Events and Information	Remarks and references to Appendices
1915 August 1 CAMBRIN.	Battalion still holding the Keeps in the line immediately S. of the BETHUNE – LA BASSEE Road.	
2. 3. 4. 5.	During the whole of this period the Battalion has been in close support to the firing line, finding parties for KEEPS situated at the junction of the main communication trenches into the fire trenches. These Keeps have been provided with means of defence so situated between both front trench and communication to enable them to hold out for two days in the event of their being surrounded. The work the Battalion has done has been the improving of communication trenches, Keeps, farms them with bricks and generally making preparation for the winter.	
6.	The Battalion has received by the Northampton Regiment and moved to billets in the BRET Rue Camp near NORDEN at FOUQUIÈRES in the Camp is being made fire with timber and canvas, and an extensive scheme of drainage is being undertaken. A swimming Bath has	

[signature]
Captain

WAR DIARY

or

INTELLIGENCE SUMMARY

(Erase heading not required.)

Instructions regarding War Diaries and Intelligence Summaries are contained in F. S. Regs., Part II. and the Staff Manual respectively. Title pages will be prepared in manuscript.

Hour, Date, Place	Summary of Events and Information	Remarks and references to Appendices
1915		
August 6. (cont.)	has provided, made by a large hole dug in the ground filled by a Mician and covered with sand bags.	
BRET RIVER CAMP NEAR FOUQUIERES		
7.		
8.		
9.		
10.		
11.	During the past week the Battalion has practised Musketry with both Rifle and Machine Guns, and has carried on the work of completing the Camp, YARDEN CITY. It is becoming evident, however, that the Camp is badly situated and will probably be moved in the Winter. The large drainage of water has commenced. Officers have to take Commands elsewhere to times the work of training the Junior ranks to take their places continues to be very arduous.	
12.	The Battalion moved into Trenches immediately N. of the	

[signature]
Capt.

1247 W 3299 200,000 (E) 8/14 J.B.C. & A. Forms/C. 2118/11.

WAR DIARY
— or —
INTELLIGENCE SUMMARY.

(Erase heading not required.)

Instructions regarding War Diaries and Intelligence Summaries are contained in F. S. Regs.; Part II. and the Staff Manual respectively. Title pages will be prepared in manuscript.

Hour, Date, Place	Summary of Events and Information	Remarks and references to Appendices
1915 August 12. (Cont.)	Road from VERMELLES to HULLUCH lies beyond the Chapel of the Notre Dame de la Consolation, which it occupied before. Headquarters of the Battalion being near the Chapel in the Rue, which is under construction. Two Companies are in the Firing Line, one in Support, and one immediately in Reserve. Lieutenant-Colonel B.C. Green having proceeded to Hospital, and Major James Young having proceeded to Scotland on short leave, Major H.C.K. Green becomes Commander of the Battalion.	
13. VERMELLES.	Owing to the difficulty of evening that all visible Patrols shall be shot, and that every man shall know when our own Patrols are going out and coming in. It is arranged that no Battalion must be sent without instructions from Battalion H.Q. who informs the Officers Commanding the Battalions on either flank.	

[signature] [illegible]
Capt [illegible]

1247   W 3299   200,000   (E)   8/14   J.B.C. & A.   Forms/C. 2118/11.

Army Form C. 2118.

Instructions regarding War Diaries and Intelligence Summaries are contained in F. S. Regs., Part II. and the Staff Manual respectively. Title pages will be prepared in manuscript.

WAR DIARY

of

INTELLIGENCE SUMMARY

(Erase heading not required.)

LONDON SCOTTISH (4)

Hour, Date, Place	Summary of Events and Information	Remarks and references to Appendices
1915. August 13. (Cont.)	What was proposed to be done that night. The Scheme of Defence in this special section was that, in the event of an attack from the support Company moved at once to the Headquarters of the Right Company and another Platoon from the Support Company to the Headquarters of the Left Company. The remaining 2 Platoons of the Support Company went to at one detach a certain number of bombing parties to station themselves at a run of important junctions in the Communication Trenches in order to deny them to the Enemy in case of a break through. The remainder of the Support Coy. to be at the disposal of its Commander to deliver a counter attack wherever he considered it advisable, and to report any action he had taken to the Battalion Commander. The Reserve Company at VERMELLES on to be at once	

WAR DIARY

or

INTELLIGENCE SUMMARY

(Erase heading not required.)

LONDON SCOTTISH. (5)

Instructions regarding War Diaries and Intelligence Summaries are contained in F. S. Regs., Part II. and the Staff Manual respectively. Title pages will be prepared in manuscript.

Hour, Date, Place	Summary of Events and Information	Remarks and references to Appendices
1915 August 13th (Cont.)	By the greatest notion which the Commander considers will favourably protect his men from enemy Casualties to Battalion Headquarters to be available from the disposal of the Battalion Commander as to Trenches available. The Trenches are divided into areas for the cleaning of which each Company is responsible.	
14.		
15.		
16.	Four Candidates from the Officers Training School at BLENDECQUES joined the Battalion for trench town instruction.	
17.	Lt. Colonel D. Laidlaw, Hot. Highland Light Infantry is attached to the Battalion for 3 days to gain experience to work in the Trenches. He Battalion is shot in England. The Company of the 5th Berkshire Regiment is attached.	

(Cumberstorr) Capt Adjt.

WAR DIARY
or
INTELLIGENCE SUMMARY

(Erase heading not required.)

LONDON SCOTTISH (6)

Instructions regarding War Diaries and Intelligence Summaries are contained in F. S. Regs., Part II. and the Staff Manual respectively. Title pages will be prepared in manuscript.

Hour, Date, Place	Summary of Events and Information	Remarks and references to Appendices
1915. August 17 (Cont.)	to the Battalion for 2 days. It is understood that this Battalion is to join the 1st Brigade in place of one of the Guards Battalions	
18.		
19.	The following Memorandum re Machine Guns was issued:—	
20.	1. The Gun is to be the absolute minimum but should be left with any one Gun so that this oft-in exceptional circumstances. Working parties can easily be found by Companies under the supervision of the Machine Gun Officer or N.C.O. These should be asked for by M.G.O. through H.Q.	
	2. Machine Gun detachments to remain O.C. Coy in close touch. Responsible for the following: Cleanliness of the standing guns, Order, and instruction in Pistols. Discipline and ...	
	They are under the Machine Gun Officer for the following:—	

Army Form C. 2118.

WAR DIARY
— or —
INTELLIGENCE SUMMARY

(Erase heading not required.)

Instructions regarding War Diaries and Intelligence
Summaries are contained in F. S. Regs., Part II.
and the Staff Manual respectively. Title pages
will be prepared in manuscript.

Hour, Date, Place	Summary of Events and Information	Remarks and references to Appendices
1915. August 20th (Cont)	The tactical dispositions had orders, keeping had retired.	

WAR DIARY

or

INTELLIGENCE SUMMARY.

(Erase heading not required.)

Instructions regarding War Diaries and Intelligence
Summaries are contained in F. S. Regs., Part II.
and the Staff Manual respectively. Title pages
will be prepared in manuscript.

Hour, Date, Place	Summary of Events and Information	Remarks and references to Appendices
1915. August 27th Cont.	August 27th 1915. Having been ordered to assume Command of another Brigade I am obliged with regret to take leave of the 1st Battalion of the LONDON SCOTTISH. I am very happy to have been associated for nearly 9 months with the Battalion & I want to thank all ranks for the cheerful manner in which they have always performed the very varied work which has fallen to their lot. Numbers of you are more accustomed to banking with your heads than with your hands. Yet you have carried out the heavy digging and disagreeable fatigues and inapproachable work in billets with a thoroughness which any other troops would do well to imitate. I wish you would have worked to have a chance at the enemy and to a really big thing to avenge your Comrades who fell at MESSINES and Neuve ... and I regret that this chance did	

Macdonald
Capt? ...

Army Form C. 2118.

LONDON SCOTTISH (9).

WAR DIARY
or
INTELLIGENCE SUMMARY

(Erase heading not required.)

Instructions regarding War Diaries and Intelligence Summaries are contained in F. S. Regs., Part II. and the Staff Manual respectively. Title pages will be prepared in manuscript.

Hour, Date, Place	Summary of Events and Information	Remarks and references to Appendices
1915 August 31st (Cont.)	not fail to you but while under my Command. Our duty has been a less glorious one, but you have exacting and equally necessary, and in the continuous strain and weary monotony of trench life in order and common you have shewn a maintained and improved your efficiency. The Army owes you a debt of gratitude for the number of officers you have sent out to it. The great number of those who, when they might have been commissioned, preferred to remain in the ranks of the Battalion is sufficient evidence of your fine Regimental spirit. I am sorry that owing to the Battalion being in the trenches I cannot say goodbye to you on parade. So I must regretfully bid you farewell by means of this letter. Believe me that the Battalion will always	

1247 W 3299 200,000 (E) 8/14 J.B.C. & A. Forms/C. 2118/11.

WAR DIARY

or

INTELLIGENCE SUMMARY

(Erase heading not required.)

Instructions regarding War Diaries and Intelligence
Summaries are contained in F. S. Regs, Part II.
and the Staff Manual respectively. Title pages
will be prepared in manuscript.

Hour, Date, Place	Summary of Events and Information	Remarks and references to Appendices
1915. August 21st. (Cont.)	have a very great spirit in his affection and regard your luck to you wherever you may be. (Signed) H. C. LOWTHER, Brig. Gen. Commanding 1st Guards Bde. The Battalion was relieved except for one company on the left by the 6th Royal Scots Fusiliers, and the Battalion moved to the left into a various part of front opposite Fort HOHENZOLLERN.	
22.		
23.	Operation Order 278/15. Operation 1. A working party of the LONDON SCOTTISH is to go out tonight at 9 p.m. from support near BOYAU 18. Similar parties will be found on the front of ½ and ½. The Brown swing park will also be out. 2. The London Scottish working party will be found by 2 platoons of D. Coy under command O. C. Coy. Conference of D. Coy commander of an officer. One platoon will be at BUCKINGHAM GATE.	

[signature] Capt RSM

1247 W 3299 200,000 (E) 8/14 J.B.C. & A.   Forms/C. 2118/11.

WAR DIARY
or
INTELLIGENCE SUMMARY.

(Erase heading not required.)

LONDON SCOTTISH (11)

Instructions regarding War Diaries and Intelligence Summaries are contained in F. S. Regs., Part II. and the Staff Manual respectively. Title pages will be prepared in manuscript.

Hour, Date, Place	Summary of Events and Information	Remarks and references to Appendices
1915 August 23. (Cont)	By 9.15 pm. meeting by HULLUCH ALLEY. Separate instructions will be sent to O.C. Coy. Capital Row. 3. Each man of the working party will carry 1 pick and 1 shovel. D Coy Platoons will draw their tools from Brigade Reserve. (The tools required may be drawn from a Reserve which has been formed near the junction of Central Communication Trench and Reserve Trench. 4. Working party will carry full equipment (including bayonet), two turnover, water bottle, and Entrenching tools. 5. A. B. and D. Coy. will each detail 1 H.C.O. and 4 men to report to O.C. Covering Party. Royal posts... at junction of CURLEY CRESCENT and CHAPEL ALLEY at 9 pm. 6. D. Coy. less 2 Platoons will take over the trenches at Support Coy. from 8.45 pm. They will take in position.	

Commanding
Captain

1247 W 3299 200,000 (E) 8/14 J.B.C. & A.   Forms/C. 2118/11.

WAR DIARY

or

INTELLIGENCE SUMMARY

(Erase heading not required.)

Instructions regarding War Diaries and Intelligence Summaries are contained in F. S. Regs., Part II. and the Staff Manual respectively. Title pages will be prepared in manuscript.

Hour, Date, Place	Summary of Events and Information	Remarks and references to Appendices
1915 August 23. (Cont.).	in billings near Battalion Headquarters as hitherto. D. Coy. will find a fatigue party to carry off rations in accordance with instructions already issued. 7. Special Stretcher Parties have been formed and will be placed by the M.O. near to head of Boyan 18. 8. While working parties are out digging will take place unless actually necessary in rear to repel an attack. Return of Working Party will be notified by Battalion Headquarters. Each Company will detail 2 of their Stretcher Bearers to report to M.O. at the Dressing Station at 4 p.m. They will as such until 5 a.m. on the 24th under orders Each Company will detail 2 other men as temporary Stretcher Bearers to complete their Squad. These will detail Bearers to report to the M.O. at the Dressing Station at 4 p.m. to act under him as Stretcher Bearers until 5 a.m. on 24th. On their way through VERMELLES the Bearers will take out stretchers from the Medical Cart leaving them up with them. The M.O. or a relieve	

1247 W 3299 200,000 (E) 8/14 J.B.C. & A. Forms/C. 2118/11.

Michael Walter
Capt. RAMC

Army Form C. 2118.

WAR DIARY
—or—
INTELLIGENCE SUMMARY

(Erase heading not required.)

LONDON SCOTTISH (1/?)

Instructions regarding War Diaries and Intelligence Summaries are contained in F. S. Regs., Part II. and the Staff Manual respectively. Title pages will be prepared in manuscript.

Hour, Date, Place	Summary of Events and Information	Remarks and references to Appendices
1915 August 23 (Cont.)	the Success of all the new detailed facts and we him as above after 5 a.m. on 24th of the Enemies is terrible.	
24.	Preparations that night were astonishing throughout. Fire was put on the whole frontage from the CHAPEL = HAISNES Road as far South as the PUTWICH Road, at least 300 yards in advance of our trench. Portion portion of the Royal Scots Fusiliers Graduated 300 yards I think [?] trench and the London Scottish Graduated 110 yards of trench. The late by Mining wire in no chosen in attacked places. Battalion was relieved by 2nd ROYAL SUSSEX REGT. and now marched back to VERQUIN.	
25 – 30. VERQUIN.	Battalion has been doing what work and also practising Musketry and Bombing during the past week.	

1247 W 3299 200,000 (E) 8/14 J.B.C. & A. Forms/C. 2118/11.

WAR DIARY

— or —

INTELLIGENCE SUMMARY

(Erase heading not required.)

Instructions regarding War Diaries and Intelligence Summaries are contained in F. S. Regs., Part II. and the Staff Manual respectively. Title pages will be prepared in manuscript.

Hour, Date, Place	Summary of Events and Information	Remarks and references to Appendices

1915 August. 31.	Battalion moved up to Reserve at LESPESSES.
	
	Sketches are attached of inventions by Pte. T.E. DUFFUS of this Battalion.
	
	  I. Bomb Carrier
	  II. Track Decline Carrier
	
	... of the Trenches. strength operator Carrier ... ... i Clark
	
	and orders bright of 23rd ...
	
	The information managed ... Ballantine and distinguished ... to the Gen have been confined by his Imperial Majesty the Emperor of Russia:—
	Cross of the Order of St. George 4th Class:— No. 253. Cpl. Sergeant.
	  Major Robert William Emslie.
	Medal of the Order of St. George 4th Class:— No. 167 Corporal Douglas
	  Alexander Stewart.	

		[signature] Captn

1247 W 3299 200,000 (E) 8/14 J.B.C. & A.   Forms/C. 2118/11.

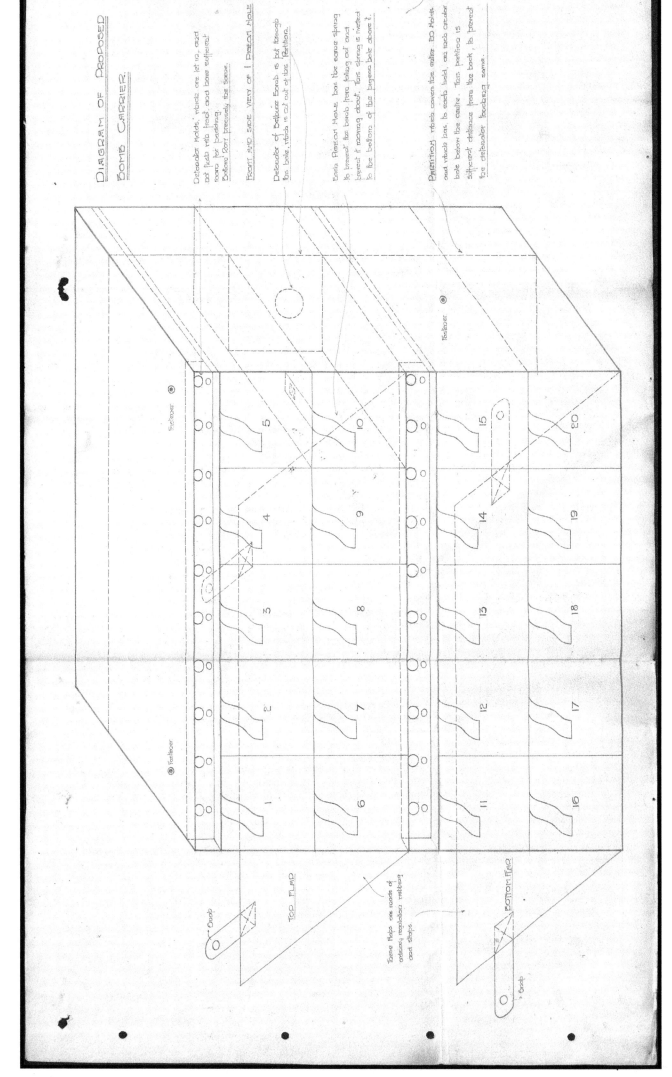

DIAGRAM OF PROPOSED
BOMB CARRIER.

Detonator Holds, which are let in, and
not flush with Hook and have sufficient
room for loading.
Bellows Roof precisely the same.

FRONT AND SIDE VIEW OF 1 PIGEON HOLE

Detonator of Bellows Bomb is put through
this hole, which is cut out of this Partition.

Each Pigeon Hole has the same spring
to prevent the bomb from falling out and
prevent it moving about. This spring is riveted
to the bottom of the pigeon hole above it.

PARTITIONS which covers the entire 20 Holes
and which lets to each Hold, are tack circular
hole below the centre. This partition is
sufficient distance from the bomb, to prevent
the detonator touching same.

Fastener

Fastener

5   10   15   20
4   9   14   19
3   8   13   18
2   7   12   17
1   6   11   16

Fastener

Fastener

Snap

TOP FLAP

These Flaps are made of
ordinary regulation webbing
and straps.

BOTTOM FLAP

Snap

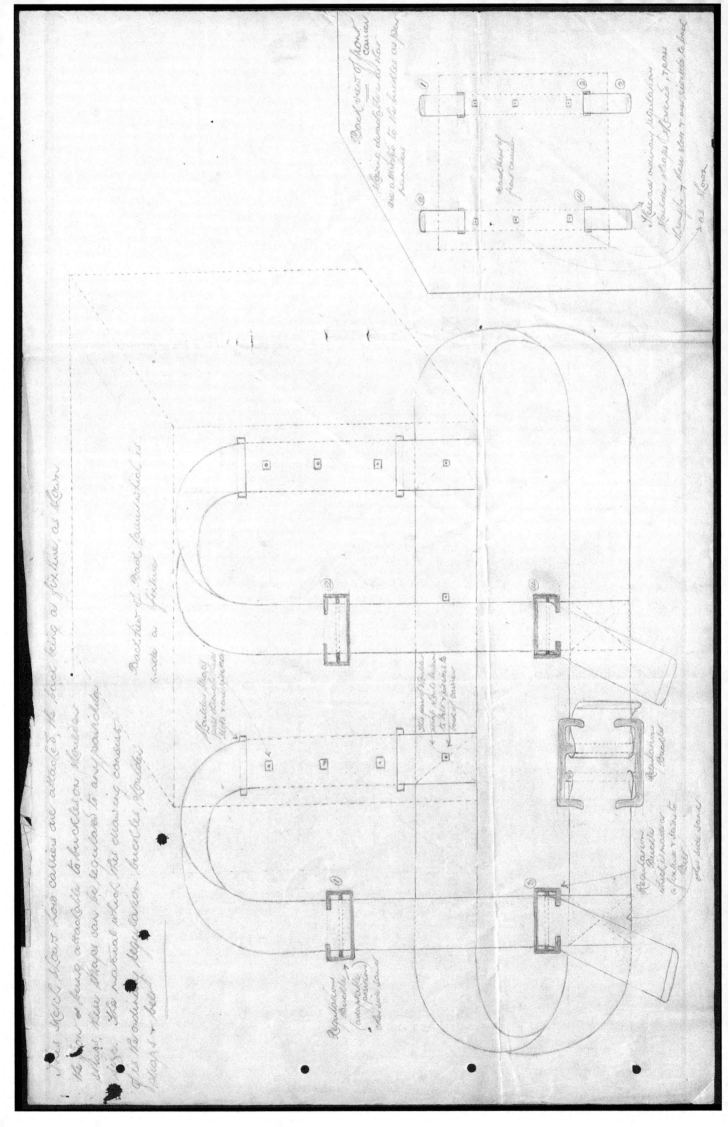

PLAN

PROPOSED "DIXIE - CARRIER"
SCALE - 5 INCHES = 1 FOOT

SECTION A.B.

Invented by
Pte T.E Druffen
London Scottish

Aug. 1915.

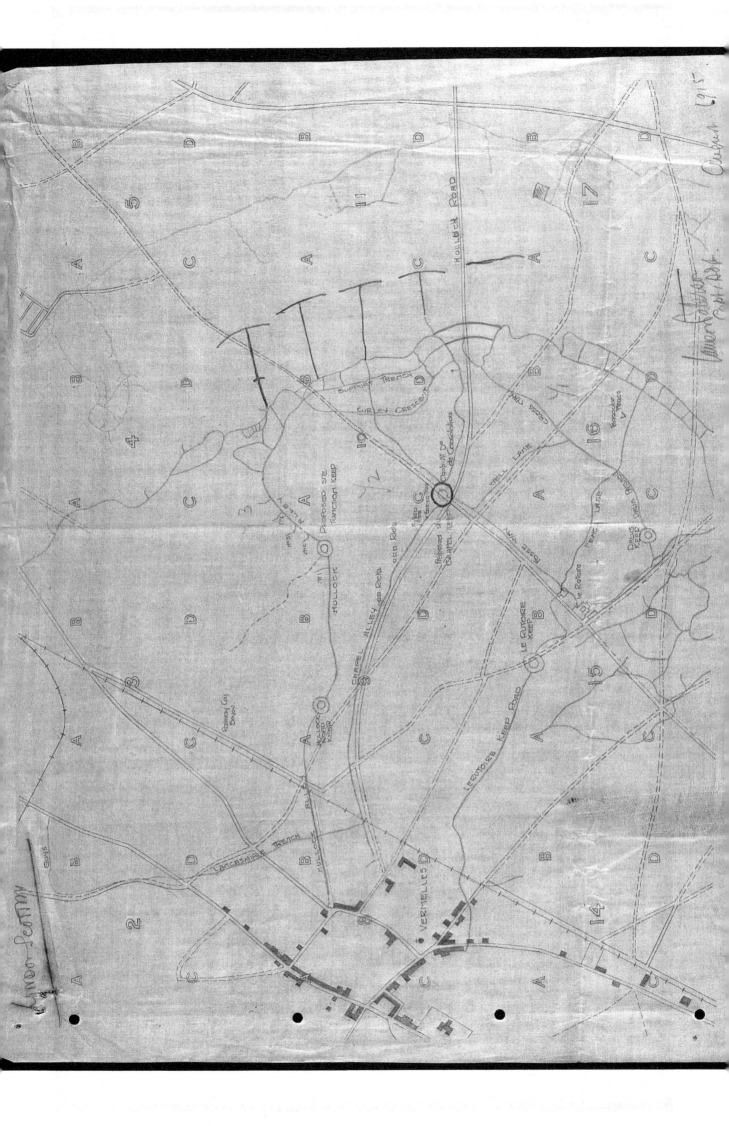

4 /st Brigade.

WAR DIARY

OF

London Scottish

SEPTEMBER 1915

Attached:-
Recommendations.
Tracing.

3

Army Form C. 2118.

WAR DIARY

—or—

INTELLIGENCE SUMMARY.

(Erase heading not required.)

LONDON SCOTTISH

Instructions regarding War Diaries and Intelligence
Summaries are contained in F.S. Regs., Part II.
and the Staff Manual respectively. Title pages
will be prepared in manuscript.

Hour, Date, Place	Summary of Events and Information	Remarks and references to Appendices
1915		
Sep. 1st 2nd 3rd LES PESSES	The Battalion is in training at LESPESSES near LILLERS. I am standing forms. are issued a more serviceable article than the flangers? We attempt to take modes smoothing the trenches to be pulled down men the era for sleeping at night. Blue lines retained and now are added for distinction	✗
Sep. 4 to Sep. 6th LES PESSES	Training. Colonel (Temp. Brig. Gen.) E.A.E. Hollond C.B. M.V.O. D.S.O. assumed command of the 1st Divn. on 5th Sept. with the Lieutenant of Major General. Summons Sesshi were held. this crowd of a ... stops piece of metal with summons point to surround the ... tonight. there are not forced to be of any value as the eye by seeing the summons point is evident. We are able to use the foresight in foretaste in object. The Machine Gun officers and under officers and N.C.O.s in turn to five Machine Gun	

(D 29 6) W 2794 100,000 8/14 H W V   Forms/C. 2118/11.

WAR DIARY
or
INTELLIGENCE SUMMARY.

(Erase heading not required.)

London Scottish

Instructions regarding War Diaries and Intelligence Summaries are contained in F.S. Regs., Part II. and the Staff Manual respectively. Title pages will be prepared in manuscript.

Hour, Date, Place	Summary of Events and Information	Remarks and references to Appendices
1915		
Sep. 7th Leptesseo	Men with knowledge of Chemistry are sent to join the R.E. at HELFAUT to make Gas. Bombing practice is carried out; there are 32 men detailed to act as bombers in each Company but nearly every man (rifle) in the battalion has now been taught how to throw a bomb.	
Sep. 9th Leptesseo	The attack from a Trench on other Trenches is practiced by the Battalion. The new tube Gas helmet (was used in this attack and it was found that the men could not run more than 120 yards) and still be fresh work the helmet on the face again was adopted that wherever the helmet were necessary that they should be rolled up on the head and only drawn down when in contact with fumes or as a precaution before entering the enemies trenches.	

[signature] Capt.

(9 29 6) W 2794 100,000 8/14 H W V   Forms/C. 2118/11.

Army Form C. 2118.

London SCOTTISH

WAR DIARY
—or—
INTELLIGENCE SUMMARY.

(Erase heading not required.)

Instructions regarding War Diaries and Intelligence
Summaries are contained in F.S. Regs., Part II.
and the Staff Manual respectively. Title pages
will be prepared in manuscript.

Hour, Date, Place	Summary of Events and Information	Remarks and references to Appendices
1915		
Sep. 9th Continued	Men belonging to Brigade Mining Party leave for special instruction.	
Sep. 10. 11. 12	Company training	
Sep. 13 & 14th	Battalion training. Daggers are issued to bombers. They are rather crude but they are issued as an extra weapon to those men should they lose their rifles and bayonets.	
Sep. 15th	Companies practice the attack in conjunction with bombers.	
Sep 16th	This is the anniversary of the Landing of the Battalion in France. A Battalion Order was held and the following telegram sent to our old Commander Lt. Col. G.A. Malcolm "on the occasion of the anniversary of our landing in France we send this token of affection and respect from officers, N.C.O.'s and men of your	

Army Form C. 2118.

WAR DIARY
or
INTELLIGENCE SUMMARY.

(Erase heading not required.)

Instructions regarding War Diaries and Intelligence Summaries are contained in F.S. Regs., Part II. and the Staff Manual respectively. Title pages will be prepared in manuscript.

LONDON SCOTTISH

Hour, Date, Place	Summary of Events and Information	Remarks and references to Appendices
1915 Sep. 16th	1st Battalion LONDON SCOTTISH. The Battalion has now been issued with additional articles for use in our coming attack. Billhooks (one to roughly every charges to carry water, flags etc. A spade in addition is ordered for today. The Knapsack is dispensed with today and in this order with the straps of sled notes and strapped on the belt, and the pack being discarded. A new bandolier has been issued to carry ammunition which is a much better pattern than the one already used; it has a flap which prevents the bombs from falling out in the carriers arms. Company Training. During the last few weeks documents and	
Sep. 17 to Sep. 20th September.		

(9 29 6) W 2704 100,000 8/14 H W V Forms/C. 2118/11.

Army Form C. 2118.

WAR DIARY

—or—

INTELLIGENCE SUMMARY.

(Erase heading not required.)

LONDON SCOTTISH

Instructions regarding War Diaries and Intelligence
Summaries are contained in F. S. Regs., Part II.
and the Staff Manual respectively. Title pages
will be prepared in manuscript.

Hour, Date, Place	Summary of Events and Information	Remarks and references to Appendices
1915		
Sep. 17/18 Sep. 20" (Cont'd) Leghem	papers more or less "Secret" are being received from the Brigade & Division concerning future operations which kept the Battalion Headquarters very busy.	
Sep. 21st Leghem	Order to Green and Battalion move to Trivime or LE MARÉQUET wood. Fighting kit is worn with addition of the packs which are to be eventually dumped before final move to the trenches. 50 extra Stretcher bearers have been told off by each Company, the rifles of these men handed over to the armourer Sergeant	

(9 29 6) W 2794 100,000 8/14 H W V   Forms/C. 2118/11.

Army Form C. 2118.

WAR DIARY

— or —

~~INTELLIGENCE SUMMARY.~~

(Erase heading not required.)

LONDON SCOTTISH

Instructions regarding War Diaries and Intelligence
Summaries are contained in F.S. Regs., Part II.
and the Staff Manual respectively. Title pages
will be prepared in manuscript.

Hour, Date, Place	Summary of Events and Information	Remarks and references to Appendices
1915		
Sep. 23rd VERQUIN	On the night of 23rd the Battalion marched to a bivouac near VERQUIN.	
Sep. 24th VERQUIN	The move at 9.30 p.m. by a special trail across country to Joose way. Before starting Packs were dumped and taken over by the Quarkmaster.	
Sep. 25th VERMELLES FOSSE WAY.	The LONDON SCOTTISH together with the 9th KINGS LIVERPOOL and a Signal section R.E.s etc. formed GREENS FORCE. This force was to form the connecting link between the 1st and 2nd BRIGADES who were attacking on divergent frontages. 1st BRIGADE on the left. 2nd BRIGADE on the right. It was the duty of each Brigade to send bombing parties from their right and left respectively to front inwards, clear the system of enemies trenches and meet at a given point, a signal was then to be sent to GREENS FORCE. The Battalion went into FOSSE WAY reporting arrived at 1.35 a.m.	
1.35 A.M.		LSP? 25d
		[signature] Lt. Col.
		OC LSH

(9 29 6) W 2794 100,000 8/14 H W V Forms/C. 2118/11.

WAR DIARY
or
INTELLIGENCE SUMMARY.
(Erase heading not required.)

Instructions regarding War Diaries and Intelligence
Summaries are contained in F.S. Regs., Part II.
and the Staff Manual respectively. Title pages
will be prepared in manuscript.

1915

Hour, Date, Place	Summary of Events and Information	Remarks and references to Appendices
Sept. 25th VERMELLES FOSSE WAY	I have only been able to draw on reconnoitred	L.S. Pl. 25th
	Stayed from the 75th Brigade.	
1.40 A.M.	The following message received from Col Green Commanding GREEN'S FORCE. "Operation Order No.1 Rolls Good. Weather forecast favourable.	E1 25th
4°c A.M.	Hour to Zero will be notified later.	
	First Division wires :- "Zero is five fifty. Inform any officers of 187 Coy. R.E. in your area." Acknowledged on envelope.	D16 25th
4.30 A.M.	Operation Order issued as follows, N°G.S. Benedum LONDON SCOTTISH 25.9.15	G5. 25th
4.50 a.m.	Order by Major J.H. Lindsay Commanding LONDON SCOTTISH 25.9.15	
	Para 1 Information. The first objective of GREEN'S FORCE until be the line 82 - 86 - 31 - 52. Having established itself on his position it is to	

Cameron Keller
Capt Adj

(9 29 6) W 2704 100,000 8/14 H W V Forms/C. 2118/11.

WAR DIARY

or

INTELLIGENCE SUMMARY.

(Erase heading not required.)

LONDON SCOTTISH

Instructions regarding War Diaries and Intelligence
Summaries are contained in F.S. Regs., Part II.
and the Staff Manual respectively. Title pages
will be prepared in manuscript.

Hour, Date, Place	Summary of Events and Information	Remarks and references to Appendices
1915.		
Sep.t 25.th VERMELLES	(1) Watch for and more forward (immedi.) any Counter	G.S. 25.th
Fosse Way 4.50 AM	attack which the enemy may attempt to push	
	in between the 1.st and 2.nd Brigade.	
	(2) Should the 1.st or 2.nd Brigade be held up, to be prepared	
	to assist them	
	(3) After the capture by the 1.st and 2.nd Brigades of their	
	first objectives it will co-operate with these Brigades	
	in the occupation of the works on H.20.d.	
	Para II Formation On the order to advance the	
	Battalion will move forward in two lines of	
	Companies in two lines of platoons. Machine	
	Guns in rear will be with the second line of	
	platoons of the leading Companies. The Trench	
	Mortar Battery will be with the second line of	
	the rear Companies. O.C. Companies are authorised	
	to call upon the nearest section of Machine Guns	

Army Form C. 2118.

WAR DIARY
or
INTELLIGENCE SUMMARY.
(Erase heading not required.)

Instructions regarding War Diaries and Intelligence
Summaries are contained in F.S. Regs., Part II.
and the Staff Manual respectively. Title pages
will be prepared in manuscript.

London Scottish

1915

Hour, Date, Place	Summary of Events and Information	Remarks and references to Appendices
Sepr 28th VERMELLES Fosse way 6.30am	They need form A Co. on the right and B Co. on the left will form the firing line forming their own supports in the manner indicated. C and D Coys. will be in reserve and will follow the leading Companies at about 300 yards distance as the Battalion move. to the 1st and 2nd Brigades leave our old and new firing and support lines the Battalion will move (6 these lines respectively) The right of the Right Company will be on B1 and the left of the left Company on B3, the left will direct. When the Commanding Officer hears that the German lines are reported clear he will order an advance to the first objective. Movement will be over ground (left blank) Para III Zero will be at- Messengers sent after a more forward will be	Gs. 28th

Laurentalin Captain

WAR DIARY

or

INTELLIGENCE SUMMARY.

(Erase heading not required.)

Instructions regarding War Diaries and Intelligence
Summaries are contained in F.S. Regs., Part II.
and the Staff Manual respectively. Title pages
will be prepared in manuscript.

Hour, Date, Place	Summary of Events and Information	Remarks and references to Appendices
1915 Sept 25 VERMELLES FOSSE WAY	Sent along the line of FENCE WAY.	G.S. 25.
	James Paterson Capt & Adjt.	Capt & Adjt
6.57 a.m.	Message received "LONDON SCOTTISH. Don't move till you receive orders". A.H. Sykes Lt.	
7.22 a.m.	Message received "LONDON SCOTTISH. Move forward at once." From Col Green. This was acted on and all Companies warned. The Battalion immediately came under heavy machine gun and rifle fire while went. To show that the enemy trenches had not been cleared as arranged. On reaching our new and old firing and support line the Battalion is ordered to halt and reorganize, this was done below the parados.	E.5. 25.
		Lawrence Allen Capt A.O

(9 29 6) W 2794 100,000 8/14 H WV   Forms/C. 2118/11.

Army Form C. 2118.

WAR DIARY
or
INTELLIGENCE SUMMARY.
(Erase heading not required.)

LONDON SCOTTISH

1915

Instructions regarding War Diaries and Intelligence Summaries are contained in F.S. Regs., Part II. and the Staff Manual respectively. Title pages will be prepared in manuscript.

Hour, Date, Place	Summary of Events and Information	Remarks and references to Appendices
Sept. 28th	The Commanding Officer and adjutant went forward to reconnoitre. It was found that both the 1st and 2nd Brigades had advanced on our left and right, but that the trenches on our immediate front were still occupied by the enemy for a front of 600 yards on each side of the Lone Tree. Orders were received	
12.45 pm	to attack these trenches at [?] from the 9" KINGS who were then in reserve would cooperate on our right. B.Co. supported by C carried out the assault. My [?] section enabled supported by Machine Gun near B1, but found that the trenches to the Lone Tree Tree that the wire was uncut and very strong. D.Co.	
2.45 pm	at 2.45 pm was ordered to move to the left. Errard. Bois CARRÉ, and carry out a flank	

[signature] Captain

Army Form C. 2118.

WAR DIARY
— or —
INTELLIGENCE SUMMARY.

(*Erase heading not required.*)

LONDON SCOTTISH

Instructions regarding War Diaries and Intelligence
Summaries are contained in F.S. Regs., Part II.
and the Staff Manual respectively. Title pages
will be prepared in manuscript.

Hour, Date, Place	Summary of Events and Information	Remarks and references to Appendices
19/15 Sep' 25th	attack going forward. This movement was developing when the Germans opposite Col. of and surrendered; about 600 in number. Came over on our front. C. Collins straight on to 6th objective. I report on the situation was sent back to Col Green at 4.50 pm as follows: To Green's Force. Have occupied with 3 Companys line N.J 82, 86, 81. on my right. are about 40 of the 9. "KING's with a Sgt of 300 yards beyond and some troops I have not yet identified beyond that. On my left are 2 Machine Guns of the BLACK WATCH. with a Gap of unknown distance beyond. I have sent out patrols down (6 the LENS – LaBASSEE Road) about BA42; Very resist. the 2nd WELSH Regt died. along that road but with a big Sap on their right. and a smaller one on their left. beyond which are the BLACK WATCH. I am moving forward	L.S.P 30 25"
	[signature] Capt A.O.	

Instructions regarding War Diaries and Intelligence
Summaries are contained in F. S. Regs., Part II.
and the Staff Manual respectively.   Title pages
will be prepared in manuscript.

LONDON SCOTTISH

Hour, Date, Place	Summary of Events and Information	Remarks and references to Appendices
1915 Sept. 25th	to the 86, 31, 82, and my left, struck the near the BLACK WATCH. The line will be of course very weakly held. Available rifles including specialists 260 Approx. casualties 350 other ranks 3 Lieutenants James Lindsay, Major, Co. LONDON SCOTTISH.	LSP 30, 25.!
	1st Brigade r A Co. in support. 18 LINE WE OCCUPIED ——› GERMAN FRONT LINE ——› We have no reports as to the progress of the Brigades on our left and right. Up to this time our casualties amount to 6. 40 %. At about 6.0 PM. order comes from the 1st Divn. to move to CHALK PITS there to support the 2nd Brigade.	
6.0 P.M.		

James Allen
O.C.L.S.

WAR DIARY
or
INTELLIGENCE SUMMARY.
(Erase heading not required.)

LONDON SCOTTISH

Instructions regarding War Diaries and Intelligence
Summaries are contained in F.S. Regs., Part II.
and the Staff Manual respectively. Title pages
will be prepared in manuscript.

Hour, Date, Place	Summary of Events and Information	Remarks and references to Appendices
1915		
Sept. 25th	The Commanding Officer and Adjutant went ahead. O.C. is about a mile S.E. from the line we now occupy. The Battalion is able to move on. Column of fours with a screen of scouts and small parts on our left flank for protection. On arrival we are told to dig in on a line running back from the left of the 2nd Brigade to protect this flank. Later this order was countermanded.	
	The Battalion spent the rest of the night and early morning in CHALK PIT in reserve to 2nd Brigade with the exception of the Machine Guns who take up a position N. of the Pit covering the approach.	
Sept. 26th	The 2nd Brigade is relieved by 21st DIVN.	
4.90 AM	at the am. and the LONDON SCOTTISH return	

(9 29 6)   W 2794   100,000   8/14   H WV   Forms/C. 2118/11.

Cameron Kellie
Capt A/O

WAR DIARY
—or—
INTELLIGENCE SUMMARY.

(Erase heading not required.)

LONDON SCOTTISH

1915

Instructions regarding War Diaries and Intelligence
Summaries are contained in F. S. Regs., Part II.
and the Staff Manual respectively. Title pages
will be prepared in manuscript.

Hour, Date, Place	Summary of Events and Information	Remarks and references to Appendices
Sep. 26"	to our old trenches opposite Bois CARRE. The night has been very cold and wet, and the men are hungry and weary. Rations are otherwhere and served out. Date is given that the 1st Brigade are attacking HULLOCH (their first objective) and GREENS FORCE are to support them. Message from	
10.15 a.m.	1st Green to LONDON SCOTTIST "De 3rd Brigade to which are attached the 73d Brigade and GREEN'S FORCE will attack the South West of HULLUCH at-11.30 a.m. 2nd WELSH from their position G18 a x o. and G18 d 2.8. will attack with their right through H13 o. x.2. or corner of trench at South West end of HULLUCH. BLACK WATCH from G18 a 3.9. and G18 c.3.5. will attack with their left through H13 a 4.4. on trench at-H13 a 9.4. South WALES BORDERERS from G18 c.3.5. & G12 d 6.0. will attack with left on H13 b 2.8.	D 21 26th

Laurence Collin
Capt. MA Qr.

WAR DIARY
or
INTELLIGENCE SUMMARY.

(Erase heading not required.)

Instructions regarding War Diaries and Intelligence
Summaries are contained in F. S. Regs., Part II.
and the Staff Manual respectively. Title pages
will be prepared in manuscript.

Hour, Date, Place	Summary of Events and Information	Remarks and references to Appendices
1615 Sept: 26th	"GLOUCESTERS and MUNSTERS, GLOUCESTERS on right and MUNSTERS on left will advance from German line between G17.6.0. and G17.6.7.6. and Suffolk attacks of three three Battalions. When GLOUCESTERS and MUNSTERS move forward GREEN's FORCE will move into old German line with left on G17.6.7.6. and remain in reserve 1st Brigade tanking parts will make strong point at H13 a.2.6. and home to rest of it. When Hulluch trench has been made good. LOWLAND Field Co. will make strong point about H13.d.2.5. When captured, Remainder of 1st Brigade will remain in present position in reserve offering line garrisons for present. Strong point. Attack will be timed so that front line reaches road from Points No.14. 6.5. to CITE ST. ELIE. at 11 a.m. Reference above, LONDON SCOTTISH will move at 10.45 a.m. to communication	D 21 26th

(9 29 6) W 2794 100,000 8/14 H W V   Forms/C. 2118/11.

WAR DIARY

or

INTELLIGENCE SUMMARY.

(Erase heading not required.)

LONDON SCOTTISH

Instructions regarding War Diaries and Intelligence Summaries are contained in F. S. Regs., Part II. and the Staff Manual respectively. Title pages will be prepared in manuscript.

Hour, Date, Place	Summary of Events and Information	Remarks and references to Appendices
1915 Sep. 26.	Trench South of BOIS CARRE followed by 9th KINGS nearly to the old German Support trench as soon as it is vacated by the GLOUCESTERS and MUNSTERS. Left of LONDON SCOTTISH to be at G.17 c. 7.6. clear of the Headquarters of GREENS FORCE. H.Qrs. GREENS FORCE would be at a point about 30 yards South of 3rd Brigade Headquarters. The Battalion moves in extended order in two lines and occupies the German Support line, the attack has evidently failed as we remain in the German Support trench for the rest of the day and at night relieve with three companies men of various units who are holding a new trench dug by the British midway between the German front line and HULLOCH	D.21 (2) 26th

Army Form C. 2118.

WAR DIARY
—or—
INTELLIGENCE SUMMARY.
(Erase heading not required.)

LONDON SCOTTISH

Instructions regarding War Diaries and Intelligence
Summaries are contained in F.S. Regs., Part II.
and the Staff Manual respectively. Title pages
will be prepared in manuscript.

Hour, Date, Place	Summary of Events and Information	Remarks and references to Appendices
1915. Sep'. 26th.	 HOLLUCH Our new trench & Keeps → German original front line. → There is still another line in front of this that is held by our troops. Heavy fighting still goes on on our left where the enemy have counter attacked Fosse N° 8. Our line is subjected to a fair amount of shelling from the left where the enemy can enfilade.	
Sep'. 27th.	GREEN'S FORCE is now disbanded and we are once again with the 1st Brigade. Our new position is heavily shelled in the afternoon; the enemy are using a number of gas shells. The fumes	[signature] Lauenslau Capt...

(9 29 6)   W 2794   100,000   8/14   H W V   Forms/C. 2118/11.

LONDON SCOTTISH

Hour, Date, Place	Summary of Events and Information	Remarks and references to Appendices
1915 Sept. 27	for these shells cause for a short time annoyance and make the eggs smart but no cases of suffocation have occurred. The 3rd Brigade (Divisional reserve) come up at night to relieve the 1st Brigade. London Scottish move back to trenches held as reserve, of the attack (25th).	
	Message to 1st Infantry Brigade from London Scottish	LSP 26. 27th Sc 92
	27 Sept. in reply SC 92 "When the Germans surrendered my Battalion marched and captured its first objective on the 1st and 2nd line. I therefore do not know what the Germans left behind on their trenches." Further message to 1st Infantry	
4.30 p.m.	Brigade 27 "Sept. 4.30 p.m. "In area referred to are 22 German dead, and one machine Gun and 1 Mortar in front trench, four a fine machine Guns were reported to me as having been	LSP 30. 27th

[signature] Alexander
O.C.L.M.

WAR DIARY

or

INTELLIGENCE SUMMARY.

(Erase heading not required.)

Instructions regarding War Diaries and Intelligence
Summaries are contained in F. S. Regs., Part II.
and the Staff Manual respectively. Title pages
will be prepared in manuscript.

Hour, Date, Place	Summary of Events and Information	Remarks and references to Appendices
1915		
Sep. 27. a	Seen in the German front line on the 25th by my men as they crossed over. James Paterson Capt "adj". LONDON ScoTTISH.	LSD 30 27
4.30 p.m.		30
Sep. 28th	The night has been very wet. The trenches occupied by the Battalion came in for a good amount of shelling, owing it is supposed to the number of our own guns that have positions in this vicinity. The Lane one or two casualties have from shell fire.	
Sep. 29.	Shelling still goes on. The enemy has brought up more guns, a counter attack is expected and the Battalion are warned to move at a moment's notice. The Battalion is relieved at midnight.	

(9 29 6) W 2794 100,000 8/14 H W V   Forms/C. 2118/11.

Cameron
Capt/Adjt

Army Form C. 2118.

WAR DIARY
or
INTELLIGENCE SUMMARY.
(Erase heading not required.)

Instructions regarding War Diaries and Intelligence Summaries are contained in F.S. Regs., Part II. and the Staff Manual respectively. Title pages will be prepared in manuscript.

LONDON SCOTTISH

Hour, Date, Place	Summary of Events and Information	Remarks and references to Appendices
1915		
Sept. 29th	By a Guard Brigade coming up, our mines back to a mining village Les BREBIS.	
Sept. 30th	The morning is spent by the men cleaning up. Not much time is allowed for this as the Battalion arrived in the early hours and has to leave at 12.0 Noon. The Battalion took the rest of the Brigade march to NOEUX LES MINES, with a distance of 100 yards separating each Company, where the men are billeted.	
Sept. 30th NOEUX-LES-MINES	The Battalion had no opportunity for bombing during this action. Bombs were issued before going into the trenches without fuses. The firing line alone in the trenches before Starting. The Fighting dress adopted will the	

Cap RM

(9 29 6) W 2794 100,000 8/14 H WV Forms/C. 2118/11.

Army Form C. 2118.

WAR DIARY

_or_

INTELLIGENCE SUMMARY.

(Erase heading not required.)

Instructions regarding War Diaries and Intelligence Summaries are contained in F.S. Regs., Part II. and the Staff Manual respectively. Title pages will be prepared in manuscript.

LONDON SCOTTISH

Hour, Date, Place	Summary of Events and Information	Remarks and references to Appendices
1915 - Sept. 30th. NOEUX-LES-MINES.	Haversack strapped on the back instead of at the side seems the most useful way of carrying rations and necessities. The waterproof sheet was carried rolled and attached to the back of the belt by the back straps. Cardigans were worn by the men. __Billed boots__ were not used except for the dropping of grease used by the men; for this they were very useful. __Shovels__ for carrying water were not found of any use and most of them leaked. __Wire cutters__ were used to cut our own wire before the attack began and the telephone wires found in the enemies trenches soon after arrival.	

Army Form C. 2118.

WAR DIARY

or

INTELLIGENCE SUMMARY.

(Erase heading not required.)

LONDON SCOTTISH.

Instructions regarding War Diaries and Intelligence Summaries are contained in F. S. Regs., Part II. and the Staff Manual respectively. Title pages will be prepared in manuscript.

Hour, Date, Place	Summary of Events and Information	Remarks and references to Appendices
1915.		
	At the conclusion of the operations the Commanding Officer made the following recommendations:—	
	Immediate Reward	
25th Sep:	Captain Low, Cloud John — D.S.O.	
	Showed conspicuous skill & gallantry throughout the day. When ordered to attack the German trenches he led his company with great skill & when held up by the German Gun fire from both flanks in maintaining a firing line was he succeeded in although enfiladed from Machine Gun fire from both flanks in maintaining a firing line & so largely contributed to the German surrender. When the Germans surrendered he at once reformed his company and marched straight to the 1st objection. By the coolness of his leading & previous training he minimised the losses suffered by his company.	
	2nd Lieut. Marshall, Keith Hubert — D.S.O.	
25th Sep:	On the 25th Sept succeeded in maintaining communication	

(9 29 6) W 2794 100,000 8/14 H WV Forms/C. 2118/11.

Lauen Veli
Capt/D.M.

WAR DIARY

or

INTELLIGENCE SUMMARY

(Erase heading not required).

LONDON SCOTTISH

Instructions regarding War Diaries and Intelligence Summaries are contained in F.S. Regs., Part II and the Staff Manual respectively. Title Pages will be prepared in manuscript.

Place.	Date	Hour	Summary of Events and Information.	Remarks and references to Appendices
1915				
			Throughout the day not only between my Headq^rs & the Companies, but also between my Headq^rs & GREEN'S force Headq^rs. As the telephone had broken down & the trenches were completely blocked, these arrangements called not only for great skill but for great courage as they had to be improvised in the open under heavy fire.	
	26th Sep^t		Captain & Adjutant Paterson, James. — D.S.O. Shewed untiring energy & ability throughout the operations, especially on Sept. 26th: when he was of the greatest assistance to me in reorganising the batt^n under very trying conditions.	
	25th & 27th Sep^t		Lieut: Groat: George Cured. R.A.M.C — Military Cross. Shewed great courage & devotion throughout the operations. On the 25th followed the battalion closely through all stages of the attack. On the 27th having completed his work with the battalion he went on his own initiative to attend to the wounded in the neighbourhood of the CHALK PIT.	

Army Form C 2118.

WAR DIARY

or

INTELLIGENCE SUMMARY

(Erase heading not required).

LONDON SCOTTISH

Instructions regarding War Diaries and Intelligence Summaries are contained in F.S. Regs., Part II and the Staff Manual respectively. Title Pages will be prepared in manuscript.

Place.	Date	Hour	Summary of Events and Information.	Remarks and references to Appendices
1915.	25th Sept.		No.1526 Sergt. Borron Keith Stuart. —	D.C.M.
			On Sept. 25th having led his platoon to a position near the LONE TREE he crawled forward to reconnoitre. While doing so he was wounded but nevertheless completed his reconnaissance and returned to this platoon with valuable information.	
	25th Sept.		No.2871 Sergt. Bell, Edward Potter —	D.C.M.
			Led his platoon with great skill during the attack. On the evening of the 25th his Coy Sergt Major having become a casualty he took over the duties & performed them with great ability under trying circumstances being without sleep for 72 hours. Rewarded in due course.	
	25th Sept.		Captain Stirling Edward Moulague —	D.S.O.
			Led his company with conspicuous skill & gallantry during the assault under heavy machine gun fire from both flanks	
	25th Sept.		Captain Styer, Hubert Lionel	D.S.O.

WAR DIARY

OF

INTELLIGENCE SUMMARY

(Erase heading not required).

Instructions regarding War Diaries and Intelligence Summaries are contained in F.S. Regs., Part II and the Staff Manual respectively. Title Pages will be prepared in manuscript.

Place.	Date	Hour	Summary of Events and Information.	Remarks and references to Appendices
191				
			Continuous good services since rejoining the batt.ⁿ in January 1915, particularly on Sept. 25ᵗʰ. During the whole of this period he has maintained his company in a high state of efficiency.	
	25ᵗʰ Sept.		No. 8241 L. Cpl. Spencer, John William — D.C.M. His platoon Serg.ᵗ & Corp.ˡ being both wounded at the beginning of the action, took command of his platoon & led it with great ability during the remainder of the attack.	
			No. 2724 L. Cpl. Bishop, Frank Cyril — D.C.M. His platoon Serg.ᵗ & Corp.ˡ being both wounded at the beginning of the action, took command of his platoon & led it with great ability during the remainder of the attack.	
	25ᵗʰ Sept.		No. 1677 Serg.ᵗ Allan, George Miles — D.C.M. Showed great efficiency & steadiness in control of the machine Guns until wounded.	
	25ᵗʰ Sept.		No. 1811 Serg.ᵗ Carrie, David John — D.C.M. Showed great efficiency & steadiness in control of the machine Guns until wounded.	

Stationery Services Press, X 8, 5,000 7/15.

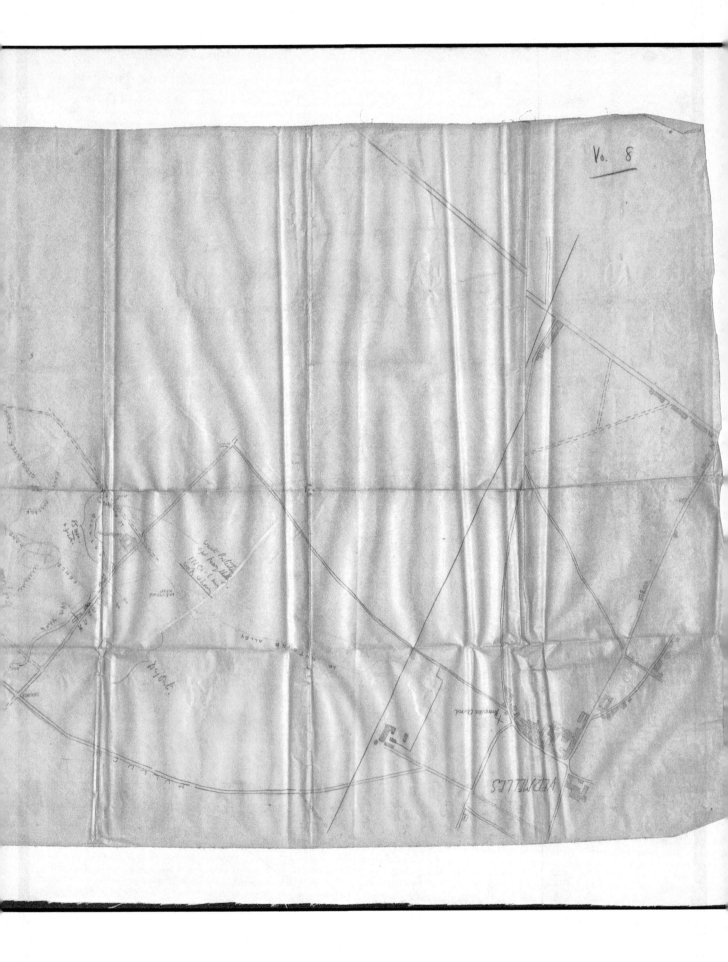

1st Infantry Brigade.

1st Division.

Supplementary

L O N D O N   S C O T T I S H

(14th London Regiment)

S E P T E M B E R

1 9 1 5

Appendices 1 to 10.
(8 & 9 missing)

Army Form C. 2118.

WAR DIARY
_or_
INTELLIGENCE SUMMARY

(Erase heading _not_ required.)

LONDON SCOTTISH H.

Instructions regarding War Diaries and Intelligence
Summaries are contained in F. S. Regs., Part II.
and the Staff Manual respectively. Title pages
will be prepared in manuscript.

Hour, Date, Place	Summary of Events and Information	Remarks and references to Appendices
1st. September 1915	Battalion & Company training at Lespesse, a village West of LILLERS	
2nd. to 20th. September, 1915 } LESPESSE.	Battalion training in the Attack — advance in the open — including Outposts, Advance Guards, by day & by night. Use of the smoke helmets and smoke bombs was taught, and the Battalion was fully equipped. Rifle Hooks, Wire cutters, Field Glasses, Daggers, Sand barriers etc being issued in addition to the ordinary equipment. During this period the Battalion attained a very high standard of efficiency. Note:- On the 15th. Sept. 1915. some rifles, as an experiment, were treated with luminous paint on the fore-sight, but when tested were found to be of no value.	

1247   W 3299   200,000   (E)   8/14   J.B.C. & A.   Forms/C. 2118/11.

Army Form C. 2118.

WAR DIARY

or

INTELLIGENCE SUMMARY

(Erase heading not required.)

LONDON SCOTTISH.

Instructions regarding War Diaries and Intelligence
Summaries are contained in F. S. Regs., Part II.
and the Staff Manual respectively. Title pages
will be prepared in manuscript.

Hour, Date, Place	Summary of Events and Information	Remarks and references to Appendices
21st. September 1915.	The Battalion moved to bivouac in Maroquet Wood near LAPUGNOY.	
23rd. September 1915.	The Battalion marched at night to bivouac East of VERQUIN.	
24th. September 1915.	Bombs and additional S.A.A. were issued and packs were dumped & put in charge of the Quartermaster. The Battalion marched at 9.30 p.m. and occupied FOSSE WAY, a trench running from the RUPTOIRE FARM to the VERMELLES/HULLUCH Road.	See Vouchers Nos. 1 & 1a attached.
25th. September 1915.	At 4.0.a.m. information was received that the weather forecast was favourable to the discharge of gas, and that Zero would be at 5.50 a.m.	See Vouchers Nos. 2 & 3 attached.
" 4.40 a.m.	Operation Orders were issued.	See Voucher No. 4 attached.
" 7.22 a.m.	Orders received to go forward.	" No. 5 "

1247 W 3299 200,000 (E) 8/14 J.B.C. & A.   Forms/C. 2118/11.

- 3 -

WAR DIARY

or

INTELLIGENCE SUMMARY

(Erase heading not required.)

Instructions regarding War Diaries and Intelligence
Summaries are contained in F. S. Regs., Part II.
and the Staff Manual respectively. Title pages
will be prepared in manuscript.

Hour, Date, Place	Summary of Events and Information	Remarks and references to Appendices
September 25th. 1915.	The LONDON SCOTTISH together with 9th. KING'S LIVERPOOL REGT. and a Signal Section of the R.E's &c. formed GREEN'S FORCE. This force was to form the connecting link between the 1st. & 2nd. BRIGADES who were attacking on divergent frontages – 1st. BRIGADE on the left and 2nd. BRIGADE on the right. It was the duty of each Brigade to send bombing parties from their right & left respectively to bomb inwards, clear the system of enemy's trenches, and meet at a given point; a signal was then to be sent to Green's Force.	
	The Battalion immediately came under heavy machine gun and rifle fire, which went to shew that the enemy trenches had not be cleared as arranged. On reaching our new and old firing and support lines the Battalion was ordered to halt and reorganize; this was done behind the parados.	
	The C.O. and Adjutant went forward to reconnoitre, and found that both the 1st. and 2nd. BRIGADES had advanced on our left and right, but that the trenches in our immediate front were still occupied by the enemy for a front of 600 K's, on each side of the LONE TREE.	
	Orders were received to attack these trenches at 12.45 p.m., the 9th. KING'S, who were then in reserve, would co-operate on our right.	

1247   W 3299   200,000   (E)   8/14   J.B.C. & A.   Forms/C. 2118/11.

- 4 -

WAR DIARY
or
INTELLIGENCE SUMMARY

(Erase heading not required.)

Instructions regarding War Diaries and Intelligence Summaries are contained in F. S. Regs., Part II. and the Staff Manual respectively. Title pages will be prepared in manuscript.

Hour, Date, Place	Summary of Events and Information	Remarks and references to Appendices
25th September 1915	'B' Company supported by 'C' Company carried out the assault by short section rushes, supported by Machine Guns, but found on reaching the line of the LONE TREE, that the wire was much strung along. 'D' Company at 2.45 p.m was ordered to move to the left towards BOIS CARRE, to carry out a flank attack, using bombs. This movement was developing, when the Germans opposite got up and surrendered; about 600 in number came over on our front. 'C' Coy went straight on to the 1st objective. A report on the situation was sent back to Col. Green at 4.0.p.m. No reports to hand as to the progress of the Brigade on our left & right. Up to this time our casualties amount to 40%. At about 6.0 p.m order comes from the 1st. DIVISION to move to CHALK PITS, there to support the 2nd BRIGADE. The C.O. and Adjutant went ahead. It is about a mile S.E. from the line we now occupy. The Battalion is able to move in column of fours with a screen of scouts and a small party on our left flank for protection. On arrival we are told to dig in on a line running back from the left of the 2nd BRIGADE to protect this flank. Under this order was cancelled by the G.O.C. 2nd BRIGADE and we	See Voucher 5ª attached. See Voucher No. 6 attached.

1247 W 3299 200,000 (E) 8/14 J.B.C. & A.   Forms/C. 2118/11.

Army Form C. 2118.

LONDON SCOTTISH.

WAR DIARY

or

INTELLIGENCE SUMMARY

(Erase heading not required.)

Instructions regarding War Diaries and Intelligence Summaries are contained in F. S. Regs, Part II. and the Staff Manual respectively. Title pages will be prepared in manuscript.

Hour, Date, Place	Summary of Events and Information	Remarks and references to Appendices
25th. September 1915	Battalion spent the rest of the night and early next morning in CHALK PIT in reserve to 2nd. BRIGADE, with the exception of the Machine Guns who took up a position W. of the Pit, covering the approaches.	
26th. September 1915	The 2nd. BRIGADE to relieved by 21st. DIVISION at 4.0.a.m. and the LONDON SCOTTISH return to our old trenches opposite BOIS CARRE. The night has been very cold & wet and the men are hungry and weary. Rations are obtained here and served out. Orders is given that the 1st BRIGADE are attacking HULLOCH (their 1st. objective) and GREEN'S FORCE are to support them. The Battalion moves in extended order in two lines, and occupies the German support line, the attack has evidently failed, as we remain in the German support trench for the rest of the day, and at night relieve with three companies, men of various units who are holding a new trench dug by the British midway between the German front line and HULLOCH There is still another line in front of us that is held by our troops.	See Voucher No.7 attached See Voucher No. 7. A attached. [signature] Capt A C [initials]

1247 W 8299 200,000 (E) 8/14 J.B.C. & A. Forms/C. 2118/11.

WAR DIARY

_or_

INTELLIGENCE SUMMARY

(Erase heading not required.)

Instructions regarding War Diaries and Intelligence Summaries are contained in F. S. Regs., Part II. and the Staff Manual respectively. Title pages will be prepared in manuscript.

Hour, Date, Place	Summary of Events and Information	Remarks and references to Appendices
26 th. September 1915.	[Heavy fighting still goes on on our left where the enemy have counter-attacked Fosse No. 8.] Our line is subjected to a fair amount of shelling from the left where the enemy can enfilade.	
27 th. September 1915	GREENS FORCE is now disbanded and we are once again with the 1st. BRIGADE. Our new position is heavily shelled in the afternoon, the enemy using a number of gas shells. The fumes from these shells cause, for a short time, annoyance, and make the eyes smart, but no cases of suffocation have occurred. The 3rd. BRIGADE (Divisional Reserve) come up at night to relieve the 1st. BRIGADE. LONDON SCOTTISH move back to trenches held on the morning of the attack (Sept. 25 th.)	
28 th. September 1915	The night has been very wet. [The trenches occupied by the Battalion come in for a good amount of shelling, owing, it is supposed, to the number of our own guns that have positions in this vicinity. We have one or two casualties here from shell fire.	

1247 W 3299 200,000 (E) 8/14 J.B.C. & A.   Forms/C. 2118/11.

Army Form C. 2118.

LONDON SCOTTISH.

Instructions regarding War Diaries and Intelligence
Summaries are contained in F. S. Regs., Part II.
and the Staff Manual respectively. Title pages
will be prepared in manuscript.

WAR DIARY

or

INTELLIGENCE SUMMARY.

(Erase heading not required.)

— 7 —

Hour, Date, Place	Summary of Events and Information	Remarks and references to Appendices
29th September 1915.	Shelling still goes on. The enemy have brought up more guns. A counter attack is expected and the Battalion are warned to move at a moment's notice. The Battalion is relieved at midnight by a Guards Brigade coming up and moves back to a ruining village – LES BREBIS. A message was received from Lt. Col. E.W.B. Green. D.S.O. saying he was very proud indeed of the way the LONDON SCOTTISH carried out the task allotted to them and of their steadiness and gallant bearing under fire. The Commanding Officer recommended the following names for gallant conduct :- Capt. E.J. Low. Sergt. K.S. Bruion. " H.H. Liger. " E.Q. Bell. " J. Patteson. " G.M. Allan. " E.M. Stirling. A/Sergt. G.J. Barrie. 2/Lt. K.A. Marshall	

Army Form C 2118.

WAR DIARY
or
INTELLIGENCE SUMMARY
(Erase heading not required.)

LONDON SCOTTISH

Instructions regarding War Diaries and Intelligence Summaries are contained in F. S. Regs., Part II. and the Staff Manual respectively. Title pages will be prepared in manuscript.

Hour, Date, Place	Summary of Events and Information	Remarks and references to Appendices
30th. September 1915.	The Battalion moved to NOEUX-LES-MINES and commenced the task of refitting.	
	NOTE. Three tracings marked Nos. 8, 9, 10 showing the locality the Battalion were in during the period Sept. 25th to Sept. 29th are attached	Nos. Nos. 8, 9, & 10 attached
	The Battalion had no opportunity for training during this action. Bombs were round before going into the trenches without fuses. The trenches before starting were any time the fighting was stopped. On the track, instead of at the side seemed the most useful way of carrying rations and necessities. The reinforcing shovel was learning rolled and attached to the track by toggle by the pack straps. Cartridges were learned by the men. Bullhooks were not worn except for the chopping of fire. For this they were very valuable. Men told off for carrying working were not found to have any use and were useless. Wire cutters were used to cut our own wire before the attack began, and the telephone wire before on the enemies trenches down after annual.	

1247 W 3299 200,000 (E) 8/14 J.B.C. & A. Forms/C. 2118/11.

A P P E N D I C E S

"A" Form.   Army Form C. 2121.

MESSAGES AND SIGNALS.   No. of Message _____

Prefix	Code	m.	Words	Charge	This message is on a/c of:	Recd. at	m.
Office of Origin and Service Instructions.				Sent		Date	
			At	m.	Service.	From	
			To			By	
			By		(Signature of "Franking Officer.")		

TO { **Greens Force**

*	Sender's Number	Day of Month	In reply to Number	A A A
	∠ S P. 1	25		

My	Battalion	is	in	position	AAA
I have	only	been	able	to	draw	one
Vermorel	Sprayer	from the		1st	Brigade

Recd.
1·40ᵐ

From	LONDON	SCOTTISH	
Place			
Time	35 AM		

The above may be forwarded as now corrected.   (Z)   *James Gateson*

                                        Censer.   Signature of Addressor or person authorized to telegraph in his name

                              * This line should be erased if not required.

8350 S. B. Ltd. Wt. W 1843/541—50,000. 9/14. Forms C2121/10.

1st INF/ BDE   Vo 1a / 15.9.15

2/Lt. GREENE DSO 2/ Royal Sussex Rt.

I have now reconnoitred the position allotted as prelim.
Battle Station and show my dispositions on
the following rough Sketch —

Z   my Signal Office

X   · HQ

M.S.   Machine Gun Section

A
B   } Companies
C
D

Mo   Doctor who Dresses —

My M.O. also has an advanced place
arranged by him with ADMS   where the
New Cut (Continuation of WELL LANE) joins the
4th Division with GLOUCESTERS & BLACK WATCH.

Note B¹ is shown in a
part of the Trench Col Green
Excludes but there are 2
big dug outs there to take 80
men which do not interfere
with free way to & fro in the
trench so perhaps they can
be included

I keep day out for Batl.

"A" Form.   Army Form C. 2121.

MESSAGES AND SIGNALS.

No. of Message _____

Prefix _____ Code _____ m.	Words.	Charge.			Recd. at _____ m.
Office of Origin and Service Instructions.			This message is on a/c of:		Date _____
_____	Sent				From _____
_____	At _____ m		_____ Service.		
_____	To _____				By _____
	By _____		(Signature of "Franking Officer.")		

TO	LONDON 9th	SCOTTISH KINGS		

Sender's Number	Day of Month	In Reply to Number	A A A
E 1	25 th		

Operation	Order	No. 1	holds	good
AAA.	Weather	forecast	favourable	
AAA	Hour	of	zero	will
be	notified	later		

From	COL GREEN		
Place			
Time	recd 4 AM		

The above may be forwarded as now corrected.   (Z)

Censor.   Signature of Addressor or person authorised to telegraph in his name

* This line should be erased if not required.

R. C. & S., Ltd., B. Wt.W3699/853. 15,000, 10/14.   Forms C2121/10.

3   D 16

LONDON SCOTTISH
~~9th KINGS~~

First Division wires :—
"Zero is five fifty AAA
Inform any officers of 187 Coy.
R.E. in your area"
Please acknowledge. so done. Envelope.

A.J.H.Dicke. Lieut

25/9/15   GREENS FORCE.

rec'd abt.
4.30 AM

Operation Orders by

Major J.H. Lindsay
Commanding LONDON SCOTTISH.
25.9.15.

Para. 1.

Information The first objective of Green's Force
will be the line 82 - 86 - 31 - 52.

Having established itself in this position
it is to

(1) Watch for and move forward to meet any
Counter Attack which the enemy may attempt
to push in between the 1st and 2nd Brigades.

(2) Should the 1st or 2nd Brigades be held up,
to be prepared to assist them.

(3) After the capture by the 1st and 2nd Brigades
of their first objectives it will Co-operate with
those Brigades in the occupation of the works
in H. 20. d.

Para II

Intention On the order to advance the
Battalion will move forward in two lines of
Companies in two lines of platoons. Machine Guns
in pairs will be with the Second line of
platoons of the leading Companies. The French
Mortar Battery will be with the second
line of the rear Companies. OC Companies are

authorised to call upon the nearest section of Machine Guns if they need them. A Coy on the right and B Coy on the left will form the firing line finding their own supports in the manner indicated. C and D Coys. will be in reserve and will follow the leading Companies at about 300 yards' distance, as the latter move. As the 1st and 2nd Brigades leave our old and new firing and support lines the Battalion will move to these lines respectively. The right of the Right Company will be on B1 and the left of the left Company on B3; the left will direct.

When the Commanding Officer hears that the German lines are reported clear he will order an advance to the first objective. Movement will be over Ground.

Para III. Zero will be at

Messengers sent after a move forward will be sent along the line of FENCE WAY.

James Waters

Capt. & Adjt.

4.50 A.M.

"A" Form.   Army Form C. 2121.

MESSAGES AND SIGNALS.   No. of Message _____

Prefix ____ Code ____ m.	Words.	Charge.	This message is on a/c of:	Recd. at 5 ____ m.
Office of Origin and Service Instructions.				Date _____
_____	Sent		_____ Service.	From _____
_____	At 7·7 ____ m.			
_____	To ____			By _____
_____	By *Manly*		(Signature of "Franking Officer.")	

TO   London Scottish

| Sender's Number | Day of Month | In Reply to Number | A A A |
| E 5" | 25. | | |

Move forward at once.

*acts or
sin ch
adv
7.22 PM*

From			
Place			
Time			

The above may be forwarded as now corrected.   (Z)

                              Censor.   Signature of Addressor or person authorised to telegraph in his name

* This line should be erased if not required.

R. C. & S., Ltd., B. Wt. W3699/853. 15,000. 10/14. Forms C2121/10.

No. 5 A

1st Objective &
LINE WE OCCUPIED →   18   86   82

GERMAN FRONT →   32   29   95
    LINE
              15

MESSAGES AND SIGNALS.

No. of Message _____

Prefix ____ Code ____ m.	Words	Charge	This message is on a/c of:	Recd. at **6** m.
Office of Origin and Service Instructions.				Date
	Sent			From ____
At ____ m.			Service.	
To				By ____
By			(Signature of "Franking Officer.")	

TO — *Green Force*

*	Sender's Number ASP. 30	Day of Month 25	In reply to Number	**A A A**

Have occupied with 3 Corps line N of 82, 86,
81 are on my right are about 40 of the
9 Kings both a gap of 300 beyond + some troops
I have not yet identified beyond that south
on my left are 2 M.G. of the BLACK WATCH
with a gap of unknown distance beyond. And
I have sent out patrols again to the
LENS — LA BASSEE Road about 13 A 4.2
they report the 2 WELCH R. just along that
Road but with a big gap on them right
a smaller one on them left beyond which
are the BLACK WATCH. I am moving forward to the
86 31 52 + my left should then be near Black Watch
available rifles including specialists: 260
approx. casualties 3 Lieutenants
350 other ranks
* the line will be drawn very weakly held

From	LENDON	Scot T H
Place		
Time	4 P.M	

The above may be forwarded as now corrected.   (Z)

Censor.   Signature of Addressor or person authorised to telegraph in his name

* This line should be erased if not required.

S. B. Ltd. W1. W1843/511—50,000. 9/14. Forms 2121/10.

Prefix ____ Code ____ m.	Words.	Charge.	This message is on a/c of:	Recd. at ____ m.
Office of Origin and Service Instructions.				Date
	Sent			From
	At 10 15 a. m.		Serial	By
	To _____ ✓			
	By _____ ✓		(Signature of "Franking Officer.")	

TO London Scottish
    9th Kings

Sender's Number	Day of Month	In Reply to Number	AAA
D 21	26		

The 3rd Brigade to which are attached
1st Bde & Greens Force will attack
the South-west of HULLUCH at 11 am AAA
2nd Welch from their position G 18 c 5 3 and
G 18 d 28 will attack with their right through
H 13 c 42 on corner of trench at South west
end of HULLUCH AAA Black Watch from
D 18 c 8 9 and G 18 c 35 will attack with their
left through H 13 a 4 4 on trench at H 13 a 4 6
AAA S W B from G 18 c 35 to G 12 d 6 0 will
attack with left on H 13 b 28 AAA Gloucesters and
Munsters Gloucesters on right Munsters on left will
advance from German line between G 17 c 60 and
G 17 c 76 and support attack of these two Batt
AAA when Gloucesters + Munsters move forward
Greens Force will move into old German line with left
on G 17 c 76 + remain in reserve AAA

From	1st Bde working parties will make strong point at
Place	H 13 a 2 6 and house to north of it
Time	when HULLUCH trench has been made good AAA

The above may be forwarded as now corrected.   (Z)

_____   _____
Censor.   Signature of Addressor or person authorised to telegraph in his name

* This line should be erased if not ____

R. C. & S., Ltd., B. Wt. W3699/853. 15,000, 10/14. Forms C2121/10.

Prefix_____ Code_____ m.	Words.	Charge.	This message is on a/c of :	Recd. at _____ m
Office of Origin and Service Instructions.		Sent		Date
	At _____ m.	Service	From
	To		
	By	(Signature of " Franking Officer.")	By

| TO { | | 2 | | |

| Sender's Number | Day of Month | In Reply to Number | AAA |

London and Field Coy will make strong point about
H 13 d 2.5 when captured AAA Remainder of 1st
Bde will remain in present positions in reserve
after finding garrisons for present strong points
AAA Attacks will be timed so that front line
reaches road from Puits No 14 bis to CITE ST
ELIE at 11 am AAA Reference above
to London Scottish will move at 10·45 am to
communication trench South of Bois ~~~~~
CARRÉ followed by 7th Kings. ready to file
into old German Support trench as soon as it is
vacated by the Gloucesters and Munster
AAA Left of the London Scottish to rest on
G 17 6 . 7 6 . clear of the Headquarters ~~ of
~~~~~~ Greens Force AAA
HdQrs Greens force will be at point about 50
yards South of 1st Bde HdQrs

From	R A Fuller		
Place			
Time			

The above may be forwarded as now corrected. (Z)

No. 7 A

HULLOCH

Our New Trench & keep →

German Original Front Line →

No Man...

Pt in 3rd.

RIGHT of GREEN'S Force.

CHALK PIT 25a.

cd Ste AUGUSTE

Fe des Mines

LOOS
TOWERS ?

LOOS Pyle

German Trench 82.

Wood 27a

ESE

ANNA

German Fort - b 20 D.

House 19a.

Rough Sketch intended to show what the view
may appear like from 17 D 8.4.
looking E.S.E.

31

53

German C.T

VENDIN le VIEL.

German 2nd line

LEFT of objective of GREEN'S Force.

LA BASSEE

S! METALLURGIQUE 54 WINGLES

1st Infantry Brigade.

1st Division.

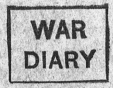

**WAR
DIARY**

L O N D O N   S C O T T I S H

(14th London Regiment)

O C T O B E R

1 9 1 5

Appendices
1 to 10.

WAR DIARY

or

~~INTELLIGENCE SUMMARY~~ LONDON SCOTTISH

(Erase heading not required.)

Instructions regarding War Diaries and Intelligence Summaries are contained in F. S. Regs., Part II. and the Staff Manual respectively. Title pages will be prepared in manuscript.

Hour, Date, Place	Summary of Events and Information	Remarks and references to Appendices
1st Oct. 1915 NOEUX-LES-MINES	The Commanding Officer, 92nd in Command, inspected the Battalion by Companies in fighting dress.	
3rd. Oct. 1915 - do -	The Battalion busily engaged in re-organizing and re-fitting	
5th Oct. 1915 - do -	The Battalion moved and took over a line of trenches from about 300 yards West of the point when the Lens/La Bassee Road is crossed by the LOOS/HULLUCH Road Northwards for about 500 yards. One Company was put in the Front Line, one about 300 yards behind it in the Support Line. The other two	
W/HULLUCH	Companies at the Battalion H.Q. were in the old German Rear Line of trenches due East of the LONE TREE. The Front Trenches were not more than 3 feet deep & the communication trenches to them had only been sketched out imperfectly. A reconnaissance & sketch explaining the position which was made two days latter are attached	Reconnaissance Report's Sketch attached tents. James Oliver Col London Sco

1247 W 3299 200,000 (E) 8/14 J.B.C. & A. Forms/C. 2118/11.

WAR DIARY

or

INTELLIGENCE SUMMARY

(Erase heading not required.)

Army Form C. 2118.

LONDON SCOTTISH

Instructions regarding War Diaries and Intelligence Summaries are contained in F. S. Regs., Part II. and the Staff Manual respectively. Title pages will be prepared in manuscript.

Hour, Date, Place	Summary of Events and Information	Remarks and references to Appendices
6th October 1915	1st. LIEUT. K. H. MARSHALL was wounded on the LENS/LA BASSEE road near the named estimate shown in the sketch under date of the 5th October 1915, as above.	Vo①, Vo②
	Orders were received in spite of this to push forward the trench on to the West side of the road. This was not able to be done owing to the presence of the enemy. As a result a trench from our Left was dug diagonally across to a point 200 yards in advance of our Right front, whereby gaining a considerable amount of ground. (See sketch drawn referred to "projected new Fire (trench)")	
8th October 1915.	Troops on our Right were heavily attacked by the Germans. A Coy was sent to their assistance	
10th October 1915	The whole of the time since we have been here has been spent in an endeavour to get food & water, ammunition & bombs, & other necessaries up to our men in the front line, also to improve communication & rear trenches. Owing to the small number of men in the Battalion this proves extremely difficult and very arduous.	

1247 W 3299 200,000 (E) 8/14 J.B.C. & A.   Forms/C. 2118/11.

Captain

Instructions regarding War Diaries and Intelligence Summaries are contained in F. S. Regs., Part II. and the Staff Manual respectively. Title pages will be prepared in manuscript.

Hour, Date, Place	Summary of Events and Information	Remarks and references to Appendices
10th October 1915.	It now becomes evident that we are intended to attack the German Trenches opposite to us in a few days. The preparations in which we have been engaged on are directed to that object.	Vol. 10 .
13th October 1915.	8 Royal Sch a the left + Loyd N Lanc (who are not beyond) guild rifles The Battalion receives orders to assault, at the conclusion of one hours discharge from Smoke bombs with which we have been provided. The assault was delivered at 2.0. p.m. but owing to the strong wind the smoke afforded very little protection. "D" Company CAPT WH ANDERSON who moved forward first, had a large number of casualties before reaching the road. Several men who tried to cross the road, were hit. "A" Company moved up in support on their right & suffered very heavily also. They were unable to get across the road. Capt. H. L. SYER himself succeeded in doing so, and reconnoitred the German wire at great personal risk, and discovered it was uncut. It was intended to cut the wire by hand, under cover of small poisonous bombs which had been sent, some of which had been distributed, but the men carrying them had been hit, and a party to go forward for	

-4-

WAR DIARY

or

INTELLIGENCE SUMMARY

(Erase heading not required.)

LONDON SCOTTISH

Instructions regarding War Diaries and Intelligence Summaries are contained in F. S. Regs., Part II. and the Staff Manual respectively. Title pages will be prepared in manuscript.

Hour, Date, Place	Summary of Events and Information	Remarks and references to Appendices
13th. October 1915.	this purpose could not be organized.	
	The fire was now found to be enfilading from back flanks, and the wind was blowing from the S.W., so that had these bombs been available, the wind would not have been in the right direction to admit of them being used.	Vo④
	Two Platoons of "B" Company went to the assistance of "A" Company, but owing to the unbroken nature of the wire & the failure of the means provided for cutting it as above described, gave evidence that the assault could not succeed without large weight of numbers, which were not available.	
	The C.O. therefore decided to remain here until dusk. Immediately after dusk, Capt. Low with C. Company & those who had not been engaged relieved the whole of the men who had taken part in the assault, who returned to their trenches to reorganize.	Vo⑤ Vo⑥

Instructions regarding War Diaries and Intelligence
Summaries are contained in F. S. Regs., Part II.
and the Staff Manual respectively. Title pages
will be prepared in manuscript.

Hour, Date, Place	Summary of Events and Information	Remarks and references to Appendices
13.th. October 1915 (9.9.pm)	The wiring party of the 3rd. BRIGADE was observed & instructed to put up wire to the left of the 3rd BRIGADE on the West side of the LENS/LA BASSEE Road, behind which line "C" Company dug themselves in. A working party of the 23rd. Field Company ROYAL ENGINEERS was sent up to assist in this & in digging a communication trench to join up with our front line. The assistance of 170 men from the LOYAL NORTH LANCS. was asked for and obtained for this purpose, together with a number of 70 men from the BERKSHIRE REGIMENT, who had become somewhat disorganized as they had lost all their leaders.	Vo ③
		Vo ⑦
Oct 14.th.	At 1.30 A.m. orders were received to abandon this work, as the Battalion would be shortly relieved by the 15.th. COUNTY of LONDON REGT. This was accomplished by 3.0.a.m. & the Regiment withdrew to the Support Line.	Vo ⑧
		Vo ⑨
	Casualties Estimated, Officers 3. O.R. 100.	

1247 W 3299 200,000 (E) 8/14 J.B.C. & A. Forms/C. 2118/11.

Army Form C. 2118.

WAR DIARY
or
INTELLIGENCE SUMMARY

(Erase heading not required.)

LONDON SCOTTISH

Instructions regarding War Diaries and Intelligence Summaries are contained in F. S. Regs., Part II. and the Staff Manual respectively. Title pages will be prepared in manuscript.

Hour, Date, Place	Summary of Events and Information	Remarks and references to Appendices
14th October 1915. (4.20 a.m.)	The Battalion moved back to the old British Trenches West of the LONE TREE, and was relieved at night-fall & moved to NOEUX-LES-MINES whence to billets in LILLERS. Casualties 1 Officer killed. 3 wounded [OR killed 7 wounded]	
15th Oct. 1915 LILLERS	The following message was received from the Col. of the 9th KING'S REGT. :- "Please accept my very best thanks for sending me your "A" Company on the 8th October at a time I was much in need of help."	
16th Oct. 1915 LILLERS	The Battalion was inspected in mass, and thanked & congratulated by the C.O. who them on the way they had behaved during the recent extremely hard trials.	

1247 W 3299 200,000 (E) 8/14 J.B.C. & A. Forms/C. 2118/11.

Army Form C. 2118.

WAR DIARY

or

INTELLIGENCE SUMMARY

(Erase heading not required.)

LONDON SCOTTISH

Instructions regarding War Diaries and Intelligence Summaries are contained in F. S. Regs., Part II. and the Staff Manual respectively. Title pages will be prepared in manuscript.

Hour, Date, Place	Summary of Events and Information	Remarks and references to Appendices
Oct. 17th 1915. LILLERS		
" 18th " "	Company Training	
" 19th " "		
" 20th " "		
Oct. 21st. 1915. LILLERS	Company Training. News received that Capt. E. J. Low has been awarded the D.S.O. for the actions described at the conclusion of the account of the action, 25th to 29th Sept. 1915, and Sergt. K. S. Bourne awarded the D.C.M.	
Oct. 23rd. 1915 LILLERS	Company & Battalion training in bombing.	
" 24th " "		
" 25th " "		
" 26th " "		
" 27th " "	Training Scouts, Signallers, and N.C.O's.	
" 28th " "		
" 29th " "		
" 30th " "		
" 31st " "	Battalion being refitted.	

1247 W 3299 200,000 (E) 8/14 J.B.C. & A. Forms/C. 2118/1.

A P P E N D I C E S   1 to 10. inc.

To. O.C. LONDON SCOTTISH   7.10.15

I reconnoitre Square 19 A this morning to
obtain confirmation of the Scouts report of
last night. From point 17 at about 5. AM
I saw a german wearing a greatcoat + with sling
rifle walking S. at pt 78 — + also what looked
like a ruined house   there

From our Fire Trench S of this point
nothing can be seen but from the shallow C.T
from our right to the Black Watch left, at
pt 19 c 5.9 I saw about 60 Germans working
at pt 76 some digging a trench on the E
side of the road. At   about 5.50 to 6.15 AM
shell fire from our guns disturbed them, some
appeared to get into a trench beside the road
other to flee across the open toward HULLUCH

I saw clear evidence of a heap of bricks +
debris as of a house that had been destroyed
at p. 78   It can be recognised by a seat
then ___ beside the main road +
by the   signpost (There is also a signpost
at p. 13 c 4 2)

From 23 0 8 2 the ruins can be seen, and
recognised by a large beam on top of them looking
at first sight like a gun.
rough sketch attached.

Ian. Peterson

8.15 AM

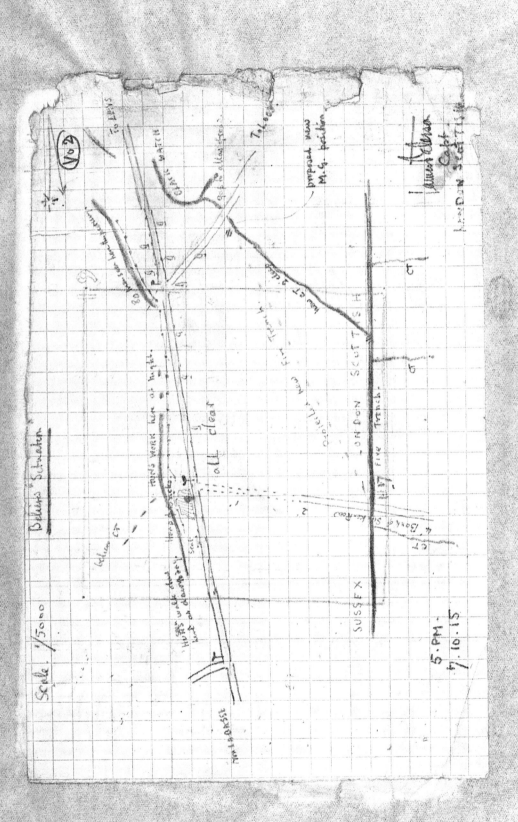

message no 2 or by hand   No 3

From OC CCO Support trench
20 Lion S.W. Trench
13.10.15 6.30 PM

I find the position here as follows

B Coy lining the road strength about 30
under Capt Anderson

Capt Syers force 20

Capt Sparks force in front line 49

My force just arrived 34

Total 133.

The Coys are mixed up & I
call them So + So's force showing
numbers under different commands as
far as I can ascertain
I attach Capt Syers report just
arrived.
I have taken command of firing
+ support line + will
hold until you order otherwise.
Clark Capt
OC CCO's.

MESSAGES AND SIGNALS.

No. of Message _____

Prefix _____ Code _____ m.	Words	Charge		This message is on a/c of:	Recd. at _____ m.
Office of Origin and Service Instructions.					Date _____
_____	Sent			_____ Service.	From _____ vo ④
_____	At _____ m.				
	To _____				By _____
	By _____		(Signature of "Franking Officer.")	

TO { **1ˢᵗ BDE.**

Sender's Number.	Day of Month	In reply to Number	
* **ASP. 4**	**13**		**A A A**

Situation my assaulting Column is reported as held up
on the West side of the road which is strongly
held on the East side. Supports are being
sent up. (2.20 PM)

Bombing in now reported (2.35 PM) as
going on in the front German line ~~opposite~~ to on
the left of my objective

Casualties

69 men have not yet taken part in
the assault. plus 10 Signallers r 12
13st 4th

From LONDON SCOTTISH

Place

Time 2.35 Pm

The above may be forwarded as now corrected.

(Z)

Censor.

Signature of Addressor or person authorised to telegraph in his na[me]

James Wilson

Capt B?

* This line should be erased if not required.

(692-2) —MᶜO. & Oᵒ Ltd., London.— W 14142/641. 225,000. 4/15. Forms C 2121/10.

Prefix	Code	m.	Words	Charge		This message is on a/c of:		Recd. at _____ m.
Office of Origin and Service Instructions.								Date _____
			Sent			_____Service.		From _____
			At _____ m.					By VoS
			To					
			By			(Signature of "Franking Officer.")		

TO	~~XXXXXX~~ 1ˢᵗ BDE

* Sender's Number.	Day of Month	In reply to Number	A A A
L S P. 9	13.		

Situation		My Battⁿ holds	the
	line	of the W side of the	road
	AAA	& the German remain	
	in their Trench	on the East side a	
	put my own	on E. side at pt 80. German WIRE uncut	
		No of men in hand 63 + 10	
	Signallers, 12 BNHⁿ. & 85 in all		
		I do not Think that if	
	I used	the men in hand I could carry they	
		objective	
List A . First report			
of Casualties	100 O.R		
	2 Lieutenants		

From	LONDON	SCOTTISH	
Place			
Time	3 50 PM		

The above may be forwarded as now corrected.   (Z)

_____   _____
                Censor.   Signature of Addressor or person authorised to telegraph in his name.

* This line should be erased if not required.

(8266-9) MᶜO. & Co. Ltd., London. W 14142/641. 225,000. 4/15. Forms C 2121/10.

Prefix_____Code_____m.	Words	Charge	This message is on a/c of:	Recd. at_____m.
Office of Origin and Service Instructions.				Date_____
_____	Sent		_____Service.	From_____
_____	At_____m.			
	To_____			
	By_____		(Signature of "Franking Officer.")	By_____

TO { **C. Coy.** repeat to & to all Commands vol 6

Sender's Number.	Day of Month	In reply to Number	
Ap 12			**A A A**

As soon as dark ~~Everything for Germ~~
~~before~~ you will 1 platoon B Coy
will relieve A, D & remainder of B Coys
& dig yourself in in or near the
West side of the road with a
post on the angle S of the road to Loos
AAA A Coy will reform in South
part of new Fire & Support Trench ~~Batty~~
3 Platoon B Coy in ~~some~~ North part
of same D Coy in old Fire Trench
AAA Machine Gun officer should report
BNHQ at once. AAA 3rd Bde Wire
Party & 23rd Co R.E. have been asked to
co-operate.

From	ADJT.	LONDON SCOTTISH
Place		
Time	6·6 pm	

The above may be forwarded as now corrected. **(Z)**

Censor. Signature of Addressor or person authorised to telegraph in his name.

* This line should be erased if not required.

(B28-9) —McC. & Co Ltd., London.— W 14142/641. 235,000. 4/15. Forms C 2121/10.

"A" Form.   Army Form C. 2121.
MESSAGES AND SIGNALS.   No. of Message _____

Prefix _____ Code _____ m.	Words	Charge	This message is on a/c of:	Recd. at _____ m.
Office of Origin and Service Instructions.				Date _____
	Sent			From _____ VO
_____	At _____ m.		Service.	
_____	To _____			By _____
_____	By _____		(Signature of "Franking Officer.")	

| TO | 1st BDE | LSP. 12. 13. 14 not addressed to you |

| Sender's Number. | Day of Month | In reply to Number | |
| LSP. 15 | 13 - | | A A A |

Situation ~~uncertain contains the~~
my Reserve Coy is relieving ~~others of~~
The others ~~much since~~ Lt EDWARDS + a party
of 23rd Fd. Co. RE have gone forward to
help. AAA My plan is to cut through
the Road at 19 C 59 to connect with 3rd
Bde Left + then to dig in Northwards along
~~forward~~ W side of road if possible as
far as 19 a 72 AAA. Are any working
parties of Reserve Troops available to
help please AAA. The CT from 24 D 49
to 19q is very shallow + has been
shelled all day + impossible in

Casualties Certainly not lighter than
already reported.

From	LONDON SCOTTISH
Place	
Time	8 PM

The above may be forwarded as now corrected.   (Z)
                                        Censor.   Signature of Addressor or person authorised to telegraph in his name.
                    * This line should be erased if not required.
(623-9) —McO. & Co Ltd., London.— W 14142/641. 325,000. 4/15. Forms O 2121/10.

Prefix	Code	m.	Words	Charge	This message is on a/c of:	Recd. at_____ m.
Office of Origin and Service Instructions.			Sent			Date_____
			At_____ m.		_____Service.	From Vo8
			To			
			By		(Signature of "Franking Officer.")	By Vo8

TO { 1st BDE

Sender's Number.	Day of Month	In reply to Number	
• LSP 18	13		A A A

Situation digging continues but men
are too tired to go on much longer AAA
Am reforming my Coys AAA German
fire makes it very hard to get in
casualties but the work is being done
well AAA. I have a Telephon at pt 19461
AAA. At 8·30 PM I got touch with L Nth
and requested them to dig a trench N from
their left to join up with me. They
at once agreed to and are now doing
AAA. May my 2 M Guns now at
24 B 27 move up to Hou in support
time about my left to enable
me to give rest to men who took part
in th assault? AAA The Bn of
140. BDE has not yet arrived

From	London	Scotton		
Place				
Time	8·30 pm			

The above may be forwarded as now corrected.   **(Z)**

_____
Censor.   Signature of Addressor or person authorised to telegraph in his name.

* This line should be erased if not required.

(698-7) —MoC. & Co Ltd., London.— W 14142/641. 225,000. 4/15. Forms C 2121/10.

11.30 PM

Capt Law reports
2 Platoon dug in Sd dgin post
+ by dawn 3 of B Cy wmbr
onhn left. 5 more Casualties
at dawn heurnhan 2 platoon
back in the pront line

Trench
Cp Law reports So Bettn
hold hui Trench into
dully

Prefix	Code	m.	Words	Charge		This message is on a/c of:		Recd. at	m.
Office of Origin and Service Instructions.								Date	
			Sent				Service.	From	Vol 9
Urgent			At	m.				By	
			To			(Signature of "Franking Officer.")			
			By						

TO — O.C. Commands — 4 Coys. *M.G.*

C.M.O.

Sender's Number.	Day of Month	In reply to Number	A A A
A S P 20	14		

The party digging under O.C. C Coy will
withdraw & rejoin their respective Coys
AAA The Trench they have dug is not to
be occupied ~~There should to be held with it~~

11.15 LONDON BN will
at once relieve the BN which will withdraw
both from 24 B 18 — 24 D 48 AAA
D Coy being on the right, then A then B the
2 M Guns will now move from 24 B 29
& the other 2 will be on the right of the BN.
BN HQ will remain where they
are.

C. Coy will inform unit on left of 3rd BDE when
they will draw from the line they were digging.

ADJ.

LONDON SCOTTISH

From	
Place	
Time	1.30 AM

The above may be forwarded as now corrected.

(Z)

Censor.   Signature of Addressor or person authorised to telegraph in his name.

* This line should be erased if not required.

(1662-9) — McC. & Co. Ltd., London.— W 14142/641. 225,000 4/15. Forms C 2121/10.

CCo

Instructions for attack   12.10.15.

1. ~~BOMBERS~~ WIRERS. The 3rd. Bde Wiring party has instruction to wire in front of the captured trenches.

2. A Coy will arrange to take over some Tools and SAA & BOMBS when they move to the German line.

   B Coy must be prepared to send a party over with further Tools SAA & BOMBS if required by D & A Coys. These men will return to B Coy.

3. Such Vermorel Sprayers as are available will be placed in the front trench. If 3 are available D Coy will have ~~2 & A the~~ other one & so in proportion.

4. BDE HQ will be at present LONDON SCOTTISH HQ, at 10 AM on 13 with an advanced report centre at G 18 d 28 after NOON on the 13th

5. WOUNDED There will be a dressing station in Conjunction with the 8th BERKS at 19 a 28 , & an aid post near the Lone Tree & LA RUTOIRE

6. OFFICERS ~~for the preparing of the autumn march that might be taken into into fields in details~~ Major GCR CROWE takes command of the 7th line Transport at 8.30PM tonight & the following Officers will report to him there at that hour

   D. JC. Brown = Constable
   W. JS Ellis
   D. F J Worlock

7. BN HQ will open at G 24 6 12 at 10 AM on the 13th

                                        [signature] Paterson
                                        Capt A[?]
                                        LONDON SCOTTISH

8.30 AM -

C. Coy.

INSTRUCTIONS for attack   11.10.15

1 Preliminary dispositions to be completed by 5 AM on 13.10.15

   D C: New Fire Trench H 19 C 69 to H 19 A 46

   A Co ˅ Supt ˅   betw. Loos Rd + junction with New Fire Trench

   B C. Old Fire ˅   from H 19 c 07 to ˅   ˅ ˅ Supp˅ ˅

   C C ˅ Supp˅ ˅ ˅ G 24 d 58 to G 05.

   2 M Gun will be near H 19 c 78

   BN HQ will be at G 24 642 , with an advanced report
                       station at   19 c 09

2. SMOKE.

   Hour of ZERO will be notified later

   D Coy will arrange to throw about 1 "P" grenade for
   every 3ˣ of front at 0.0 ; 0.15 ; 0.30; 0.40; 0.50;
   0.55.

3. General SCHEME

   D Coy is to occupy the German Trench about 200ˣ E of
   the road on the frontage H 19 c 99 — H 19 a 93 under
   cover of the end of the smoke . In case the destruction of the wire
   by the Artillery has been insufficient D Coy must
   cut it for themselves. To help in this 40 Turmite
   Bombs have been issued to it

   As soon as D Coy have penetrated the German Trench at
   any point They will send bombers outwards towards
   the flanks of their objective.

   A Coy's task is to move , on the initiative of its
   Commander ; after D Coy ___ to occupy the point
   H 19 A 90 (any D Coy men who may be there
   taking an opportunity to close to their left) &
   to make it into a strong point.

3.   General Scheme continued.

A Coy will block all C.T. running S or E at
suitable points to ensure their own protection.
The ~~Coast~~ BN Signallers have instruction to
connect the German line by wire with the
advanced Report Station as soon as practicable
(It is understood that a working party of RE has
orders to assist in the consolidation of the right
of our objective probably at dusk)

B Coy will move on the initiative of its Commander
after A + will occupy a the New Fire Trench
where it will be in support.   If operations
go favourably it is not intended that B Coy
should move over to the German line,
but O.C.B.Coy must be ready to send help to D-
A Coy if by doing so the attainment of the
~~point~~ objective could be ensured . He must
also be prepared to meet a counter attack
delivered between our right and the left
of the BN on our right

C. Coy.   will be in ~~Batt~~ Reserve. They will take any
opportunity of bringing long range overhead fire on the
enemy 1 Machine Gun will Co. operate
Trench mortar By from 9 to 10 will fire on German Trench
E of pt 80.

                                        James Paterson
                                        Capt Adjt.

10. PM.

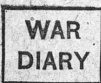

LONDON   SCOTTISH

(14th London Regiment)

N O V E M B E R

1 9 1 5

Army Form C. 2118.

WAR DIARY

or

INTELLIGENCE SUMMARY

(Erase heading not required.)

Instructions regarding War Diaries and Intelligence Summaries are contained in F. S. Regs., Part II. and the Staff Manual respectively. Title pages will be prepared in manuscript.

LONDON SCOTTISH

Hour, Date, Place	Summary of Events and Information	Remarks and references to Appendices
1st. November 1915. LILLERS.	The Battalion in reserve at LILLERS. Telegrams of congratulation on the occasion of Halloween was exchanged between the different Battalions. Waterproof capes were issued to all men. These are very excellent articles, and were badly needed through all last winter.	
3rd. November, 1915 LILLERS.	Lt. Col. G. H. Lindsay proceeded on short leave to Gt. Britain. Capt. E. J. Low D.S.O. assumes command of the Battalion.	
4/11 November, 1915 LILLERS.	The Battalion has practised Company training with a special view of bombing, including concentration of bomb force. Shooting, including shooting with the smoke helmet on, and night operations, including relief of trenches, the use of the West Bomb Thrower, etc. Instructions have been given in the protection of the feet from frostbite, and the methods found useful by the Guards	

1247   W 3299   200,000   (E)   8/14   J.B.C. & A.   Forms/C. 2118/11.

Army Form C. 2118.

LONDON SCOTTISH

WAR DIARY

or

INTELLIGENCE SUMMARY

(Erase heading not required.)

Instructions regarding War Diaries and Intelligence Summaries are contained in F. S. Regs., Part II. and the Staff Manual respectively. Title pages will be prepared in manuscript.

Hour, Date, Place	Summary of Events and Information	Remarks and references to Appendices
1/11 November 1915 LILLERS (contd.)	Division when taking Hohenzollern Redoubt with grenades. Scouts & Snipers being trained under Brigade arrangements. There has been an unusual number of concerts of all kinds and a cinematograph entertainment. Men have had hot baths.	
11/13 th November 1915 LILLERS	Battalion continues training; special instruction being given in trench duties & bombing.	

1247 W 3299 200,000 (E) 8/14 J.B.C. & A.   Forms/C. 2118/11.

Army Form C. 2118.

Instructions regarding War Diaries and Intelligence Summaries are contained in F. S. Regs., Part II. and the Staff Manual respectively. Title pages will be prepared in manuscript.

WAR DIARY

or

INTELLIGENCE SUMMARY

(Erase heading not required.)

LONDON SCOTTISH.

Hour, Date, Place	Summary of Events and Information	Remarks and references to Appendices
14th November 1915.	The Battalion entrained at LILLERS for NOEUX and marched to MAZINGARBE: rested here all day & had good dinner. After dark, Batt⁹. relieved the 6th. LONDON REGT. in the six German & British line of Trenches just north of the road from Bethune to Lens, the extreme position being between RAILWAY ALLEY and LOOS ALLEY. Boots, Gum, Thigh, are issued. Cookers & Water carts were brought into ruined houses on the LENS ROAD and hot food was therefore obtained twice daily. The chief work of the Battalion was in trying to repair	
15/16th November 1915.	the trenches which had been very much neglected.	
16th November 1915.	In the evening the Battalion relieved the 8th R. BERKS. REGT. in A.2. Sector between the Shell Pit on the road LENS - LA BASSEE & the junction of that road with the one S. of the LOOS - HULLUCH Road. The Battalion H.Q. being on the	

1247   W 3299   200,000   (E)   8/14   J.B.C. & A.   Forms/C. 2118/11.

Army Form C. 2118.

WAR DIARY

or

INTELLIGENCE SUMMARY

(Erase heading not required.)

Instructions regarding War Diaries and Intelligence Summaries are contained in F. S. Regs., Part II. and the Staff Manual respectively. Title pages will be prepared in manuscript.

LONDON SCOTTISH

Hour, Date, Place	Summary of Events and Information	Remarks and references to Appendices
16th November 1915	GRENAY - BENEFONTAINE Road. The weather was bad & a great deal of work had to be done in bringing the trenches into order. Owing to the entire absence of firing at night, troops were able to move across the open to the front line trenches, thereby very considerably relieving the difficulties of life.	
18th November 1915	The Battalion was relieved by the 6th WELCH REGT. and marched to Divisional Reserve at MAZINGARBE	
19/22 November 1915. MAZINGARBE	The Battalion engaged in cleaning up, & in cleaning the whole village of MAZINGARBE; the sanitary condition of which was very bad owing to the neglect of previous troops. It was found that men who wore Gum Boots for a longer period than 24 hours got bad feet & that men who marched even a short distance in Gum Boots suffered considerably from them. Orders were, therefore, issued to the	

2247 W 8299 200,000 (E) 8/14 J.B.C. & A.   Forms/C. 2118/11.

Army Form C. 2118.

LONDON SCOTTISH

Instructions regarding War Diaries and Intelligence
Summaries are contained in F. S. Regs., Part II.
and the Staff Manual respectively. Title pages
will be prepared in manuscript.

WAR DIARY
or
INTELLIGENCE SUMMARY

(Erase heading not required.)

Hour, Date, Place	Summary of Events and Information	Remarks and references to Appendices
19/22 November 1915 MAZINGARBE	Battalion that no man was to wear Gum boots for longer than 20 hours at a stretch & that every man was to remove his Gum Boots, rub feet, & put on leather boots, at least once daily; leather boots to be kept on for several hours.	
23/12/15 MAZINGARBE	BRIGADE in Divisional Reserve. Work, principally sanitation. Baths & refitting. Inspection of 1st. BRIGADE by Commander-in-Chief	
24/12/15 — do —	Moved to trenches. Battalion in support in the old line of German Trenches just N. & Fosse No. 7 on the BETHUNE/LENS Road.	
26/12/15 / 27/12/15	Battalion engaged in repairing trenches which had fallen in in many places on account of the wet weather, also in collecting old rifles & equipment from the battlefield	

1247 W 3299 200,000 (E) 8/14 J.B.C. & A.   Forms/C. 2118/11.

Army Form C. 2118.

WAR DIARY

OR

INTELLIGENCE SUMMARY

(Erase heading not required.)

LONDON SCOTTISH.

Instructions regarding War Diaries and Intelligence Summaries are contained in F. S. Regs., Part II. and the Staff Manual respectively. Title pages will be prepared in manuscript.

Hour, Date, Place	Summary of Events and Information	Remarks and references to Appendices
28th. November 1915.	"A" & "D" Coys. went up to Firing Line on the left of Sector. B. 2. from the Chalk Pit just S. of Pit. 14. Pois to the junction of the LENS/LA BASSE — LOOS/HULLUCH Roads.	
31st. November 1915.	Battalion relieved & went into reserve at PHILOSOPHE. The houses which had been damaged by shell fire were repaired by Pioneers. Battalion engaged in cleaning up the village & in work on communication trenches.	

1247 W 8299 200,000 (E) 8/14 J.B.C. & A. Forms/C. 2118/11.

WAR
DIARY

L O N D O N   S C O T T I S H

(14th London Regiment)

D E C E M B E R

1 9 1 5

Appendices 1 to 4.

Army Form C. 2118.

WAR DIARY
— or —
INTELLIGENCE SUMMARY

(Erase heading not required.)

LONDON SCOTTISH

Instructions regarding War Diaries and Intelligence
Summaries are contained in F. S. Regs., Part II.
and the Staff Manual respectively. Title pages
will be prepared in manuscript.

Hour, Date, Place	Summary of Events and Information	Remarks and references to Appendices
1–2 December 1915	The Battalion was in the trenches opposite the village of CITÉ ST. ELIE, its right resting on the road from VERMELLES to HULLUCH; at a point two-thirds of the way. The 9th Battery R.A. being a unit of the 15th DIVISION being on its left. The Battalion thus being on the left flank of the 1st DIVISION. Battalion H.Q. were on the crest of the hill behind in the German front line.	
	The trenches were exceedingly wet & the weather very bad. Owing to there being no shelters from the weather on the front line, men suffered a good deal from exposure.	
	Work chiefly consisted of laying floor-boards in the trenches & repair the sides where they had fallen in.	
Night of 2/3rd Dec. 1915.	The Battalion moved back to billets in the Western end of PHILOSOPHE.	
	Owing to the careless manner in which officers and men walk about the open during daylight along the old German front line. All officers will take steps to prevent this in the case of officers and men of other Brigades as well as their own."	
	Owing to the careless manner in which officers & men walked about near the trenches, it was necessary to issue the following order :—	
	"Attention is called to the unnecessary manner in which officers and men walk about the open during daylight along the old German front line. All officers will take steps to prevent this in the case of officers and men of other Brigades as well as their own."	

Campbell
Captain

1247. W 3509 200,000 (E) 8/14 J.B.C. & A. Forms/C. 2118/11.

Army Form C. 2118.

LONDON SCOTTISH

WAR DIARY
or
INTELLIGENCE SUMMARY

(Erase heading not required.)

Instructions regarding War Diaries and Intelligence Summaries are contained in F. S. Regs, Part II. and the Staff Manual respectively. Title pages will be prepared in manuscript.

Hour, Date, Place	Summary of Events and Information	Remarks and references to Appendices
PHILOSOPHE But... December 1915.	In order to avoid men coming straight out from the trenches and having to go on guard the same night, an order was issued that the guard would for the first night on coming out, be found by men of the 1st Line Transport. The following is a copy of Battalion Orders No 342 (para 15) of 3/12/15 :- "The Q.M. & Transport Officer will report by 6. p.m. tomorrow the names of 10 men now employed at the 1st Line Transport who they recommend should now return to their companies and do duty with them on the firing line. O.C. Coy will report by same hour the names of 3 men in each bay who have been out continuous by in the firing line for a considerable time and who they consider have earned a rest and who they recommend to be employed at the 1st line."	
December 5th. 1915.	The Battalion moved to the trenches. Operation Orders for this move are attached hereto as a specimen.	①

Capt Adjt

1247 W 3200 200,000 (E) 8/14 J.B.C. & A.   Forms/C. 2118/1.

Army Form C. 2118.

WAR DIARY

or

INTELLIGENCE SUMMARY

(Erase heading not required.)

Instructions regarding War Diaries and Intelligence Summaries are contained in F. S. Regs., Part II. and the Staff Manual respectively. Title pages will be prepared in manuscript.

LONDON SCOTTISH

Hour, Date, Place	Summary of Events and Information	Remarks and references to Appendices
PHILOSOPHE 4/12/15	Owing to inferiority of recent drafts joining the Battn, the following letter was sent by the C.O. to the 1st. BRIGADE. "Recent drafts sent to me from my 3rd. Battalion have proved to be markedly inferior to previous drafts sent by the 2nd. Battalion; not only in training but also discipline & morale. I attribute this largely to the fact that the training in the 3rd. Battalion is in the hands of a teaching staff composed almost exclusively of officers who have not only never served in France, but have not even accepted the Imperial Service Obligation. I consider that the efficiency of the drafts would be greatly improved if the system of exchange of officers foreshadowed in a recent memorandum could be carried out." Following on the MEMO. the names of the following Officers now serving were submitted for Exchange Capt. C.J. Low DSO Ty Capt. HC SPARKS 2Lt Ty Capt. JWD ANDERSON .	

1247 W 3299 200,000 (E) 8/14 J.R.C. & A. Forms/C. 2118/11.

[signature] Captain

Army Form C. 2118.

LONDON SCOTTISH

WAR DIARY

or

INTELLIGENCE SUMMARY

(Erase heading not required.)

Instructions regarding War Diaries and Intelligence Summaries are contained in F. S. Regs., Part II. and the Staff Manual respectively. Title pages will be prepared in manuscript.

Hour, Date, Place	Summary of Events and Information	Remarks and references to Appendices
5th. December 1915.	A specimen of Battalion Routine Orders issued on the 5th inst whilst in the trenches are attached hereto. The Battalion was in the same trenches as it was on the beginning of the month	(2)
Night 8/9 December 1915.	Battalion was relieved and moved to billets at NOEUX-LES-MINES, being conveyed there from PHILOSOPHE in motor omnibuses	
NOEUX-LES-MINES 9/13 December 1915.	Battalion engaged in cleaning up, having baths and in training in bombing. Battalion Bearers trained in use of Vermorel Sprayer. From the 10th Dec. a class of instruction for senior N.C.O.'s is held each day under the Adjutant and one for junior N.C.O.'s under the Battn. Sergt. Major.	
Night 14/15 December 1915.	The Battalion relieved 1/5 KINGS OWN LANCASTER REGT. in support. The Battn. H.Q. being in the Northern-most house of LOOS on the road from GRENAY to BENEFONTAINE	

1247 W 8299 200,000 (E) 8/14 J.B.C. & A.   Forms/C. 2118/11.

James .... Capt A.H.

WAR DIARY
or
INTELLIGENCE SUMMARY

(Erase heading not required.)

Instructions regarding War Diaries and Intelligence Summaries are contained in F. S. Regs., Part II. and the Staff Manual respectively. Title pages will be prepared in manuscript.

Hour, Date, Place	Summary of Events and Information	Remarks and references to Appendices
15/17 December 1915	The experiment was tried of attaching to the Medical Officers six men who were not very strong, and who with two Sanitary and R.A.M.C. men did duty in conveying water to men in the trenches. Ten 2 gallon petrol tins being carried to each 60 men. This proved very successful.	
Night 17/18 December 1915	The Battalion moved into the Front Line, its right being front along the road from LENS to LA BASSEE, its right 150 yds. N. of the Chalk Pit struck in N. of Pit 14. Bns. and its left being opposite the ruins of an estaminet about 360 yds. N. of the road above refered to. The 1st. CAMERONS being right Battn. & a unit of the 3rd. Brigade on the left	
Night 20/21 December 1915	Battalion was relieved by the 8th. R. BERKSHIRE REGT. and moved into billets in the 6 rows E. of Pit 14. 93.	(3)
24th. December 1915	Copy of letter is attached sent by the C.O. to 1st. INFANTRY BRIGADE re attachment of officers of 3rd. Battn. LONDON SCOTTISH to 1st Battn. whilst the latter is in the trenches.	

Army Form C. 2118.

LONDON SCOTTISH

- 6 -

WAR DIARY

or

INTELLIGENCE SUMMARY

(Erase heading not required.)

Instructions regarding War Diaries and Intelligence
Summaries are contained in F. S. Regs., Part II.
and the Staff Manual respectively. Title pages
will be prepared in manuscript.

Hour, Date, Place	Summary of Events and Information	Remarks and references to Appendices
24th December 1915.	Owing to the hardships & hardships men in the front line trenches had to undergo chiefly through lack of shelter, a letter was written on this subject to 1st INFANTRY BRIGADE by C.O. Copy of letter herewith	(4)
21st December 1915. PHILOSOPHE	A draft of 92 men joined the Battalion.	
22/3 December 1915 PHILOSOPHE	Battalion engaged in cleaning up & in finding fatigue parties to work on Communication Trenches	
Night of 23/4 Dec. 1915.	Battalion relieved the 8th R. BERKS. REGT. in the trenches from which relieved on the night 20/21 Dec. The Germans hung again on the flight and a raid of the 2nd Brigade on the left	
24/26th Dec. 1915.	In the trenches, which are still in a bad state owing to the wet weather	

Lane Talbin
Capt A.D.

LONDON SCOTTISH

-7-

WAR DIARY

or

INTELLIGENCE SUMMARY

(Erase heading not required.)

Instructions regarding War Diaries and Intelligence
Summaries are contained in F. S. Regs, Part II.
and the Staff Manual respectively. Title pages
will be prepared in manuscript.

Hour, Date, Place	Summary of Events and Information	Remarks and references to Appendices
Night 26/27 Dec. 1915.	Battn. relieved by 1/9 KINGS LIVERPOOL REGT. and moved to billets in NOEUX-LES-MINES being conveyed there from PHILOSOPHE in motor omnibuses	
NOEUX-LES-MINES 27/31 Dec. 1915.	Training as when last here.	

Cecil Dunn
Capt.M

A P P E N D I C E S   1 to 4.

Copy ✓

Operation Orders by Lt. Col. B.C. Green. C.M.G. T.D.
commanding LONDON SCOTTISH   5/12/15.

I. The LONDON SCOTTISH will relieve those of the 1st. CAMERON HIGHLANDERS
N. of the HULLUCH ROAD exclusive today.

    A. Coy. will ~~be in the support line~~ hold from the road exclusive
to the Gap exclusive; D. Coy. from the GAP inclusive to DEVON LANE

    C. Coy. will be in the Support Line with its left on DEVON LANE
B. Coy. in the same Line with its right on STONE STREET. Two
platoons of each of these Coys. may be in the Reserve Line at the
discretion of their commanders.

    H.Q. of both these Coys. will be at the Dug-out in the
Reserve Line near STONE STREET. which was formerly A. Coy. H.Q.

    The Battn. Signalling Sergt. will arrange to connect
this Dug-out by telephone with Battn. H.Q. by 9. opm.
and later on it is hoped to connect it up with the H.Q. of
the right Sub-section.

    Battalion H.Q. will be established at head of
DEVON LANE by 7. opm.

II. Advance Parties from each Coy. will start in time to reach O.C.
Coys. whom they are relieving in the trenches by 5. opm. O.C.
Coys. will make their own arrangements.

III. The Coys. etc. will parade and march to the trenches
independently at the following hours:- Signallers, Scouts &
3 Pipers at 3. opm. D. Coy. at 3.5 pm. A. Coy. at 3.10pm
B. Coy. at 3.15 pm. "C". Coy. at 3.20pm.

IV. The T.O. will arrange for a pack horse to report to the
Signalling Sergt. at 2.30pm. to take up Signalling Panniers
    He will also detail 2 limbered Waggons., 1 to be
at Battn. H.Q. at 2. opm. to receive Officers Kits &c., the other
to be loaded with wood, coke, etc. by the Q.M. These waggons
will move to PHILOSOPHE. report to O.C. "D" Coy. at 2.50pm.
they will act under his orders and precede his company to the
water tanks, at which point their contents will be taken from
them by the Coys. as they pass. Route:- VERMELLES, thence

at discretion of O.C. Coys. in or beside RUTOIRE ALLEY & WINGS WAY

V. On arrival in the trenches D. & A. Coys. will send runners to Battn. H.Q. who knows the position of their H.Q.

VI. Snipers will remain with their Companies.

VII. The Sanitary Squad will parade under the M.O's. orders tomorrow afternoon and will accompany him to the trenches.

The M.O. will select 6 men from among those whom he does not consider fit for duty in the trenches, and advise their Companies. These men will be attached to him at the Dressing Station in addition to his present staff. He will make all arrangements for the delivery of 10 petrol tins of water to each Company daily in the trenches, and 6 to Battn. H.Q. The M.O. will also see that a guard is maintained over the water tanks, and that two of them are exclusively reserved for this Battalion.

VIII. "C" Coy. will provide ration parties for "D" Coy. and "B" for "A" Coy. The Q.M. will arrange hot soup for the ration parties at the point where the cart stops; parties will take their mess-tins with them.

Ration parties will be instructed to bring down all empty petrol tins to be stacked near the tanks, and rifles and equipment from the battlefield to be handed over to the Q.M. for return.

IX. The Battn. Pioneer Section will be attached to "C" Coy. and act under the orders of O.C. "C" Coy. The N.C.O. i/c will assemble this party and report to O.C. "C" Coy. at 3.10pm.

X. O's.C. "B" & "C" Coys will arrange Bombing Parties on their flanks to be prepared to block DEVON LANE & STONE STREET should the emergency arise. 7 Bombers from "C" will be attached to "D" Coy. and 7 from "B" to "A" Coy.

XI. O.C. Coys. will prepare daily written schedules of work.

XII. O.C. Coys. will report "relief complete" as soon as they are responsible for defence of the line to which they are moving their men.

XIII. Every effort must be made to leave billets clean before the Battalion moves.

Capt & Adjt.

Copy

Battalion Routine Orders by Lieutenant Colonel B.C. Green
Cmg. T.D. commanding London Scottish   6/12/15

1 Rations Usual place, 5.30 P.M. There will be
two pack horses for each Company, a scout
has instructions to guide them from the water
tanks down the Hulluch Road, as far as
"C" & "B" Companies' Headquarters, where
parties should meet them, if found practicable
the horses will be taken nearer the front
line, north of the Hulluch Road.

2 Artillery Programme Tomorrow.

    8.A.M. PIT. 14 BIS
    10.A.M. German Front Line opposite Gloucesters
    2.30 P.M. German line opposite B.1.

3/ Work to be done. The West bomb thrower is
to be in position by Wednesday night, "C"
Company will provide a working party of
ten men for "D" tonight, in order to get
the emplacement in condition.

                    A party of an officer and 25 men
of the Cameron Highlanders will carry down 50
trench boards for "B" Company tonight starting
from the Water Tanks at 4.30 P.M. They are to be
used in boarding Stone Street, working from the
front line westwards. Latrines require attention
everywhere and there are many bombs unserviceable,
these are to be returned to Sgt. McInnes in charge
of the stores at the Water Tanks, by every
party which goes back. All empty petrol tins
in the front line are to be sent back by the
water parties to the Medical Officer. In
several places the Loop trench has fallen in
badly, these must be excavated today. Men
should not be allowed to write home while
they are in the trenches, except under exceptional
circumstances, the rifles of two men who were
writing home this morning were found to be dirty
and jammed. It is suggested that not nearly enough
use is made of the half light at dawn and
dusk, when work can be done more rapidly
than at night and without being seen by the

Germans.

4. O.C. Companies will send with their work report tomorrow a list of trench stores. This must be complete and include all those lying about, whether handed over by us to the Camerons or not, in the case of bombs it should be stated whether they are in working order or defective.

5. "D"Co will arrange tonight to bury the dead Guardsman in the northern sap and to improve the tactical position of the sap.

No 3400. H.C.Mahan, D.Co, if still with the battalion is to report to the Adjutant at 6.P.M. tonight in order to proceed home to take up a commission.

No 2466. L/Cpl. Wm. Sayers, A.Co, is appointed to a commission and will proceed home today.

Pte. J.P. Reid is appointed to a commission and will report to the Adjutant at 6. P.M. today

(Sgd) James Patterson
Capt & Adj.

(3)

24/12/15.

To: 12th Infantry Brigade

With reference to the attachment of senior officers now at home to Units in the field for a short period of instruction, I suggest that an opportunity be given to the Commanding Officer, 2nd in command and Adjutant of the 3rd Battalion of my regiment to spend a few days with me while we are in the trenches to enable them to appreciate some of the conditions for which they are to train the drafts that they are preparing to send out to me.

(sgd) G. C. Green
Lt. Col.
Commanding 1st/14th Batt Scott 1 SH

Copy

To:-

1st Infantry Brigade

(4)

Shelters in the Front Line.

Careful consideration and inspection of my men while in the front line and after they have come out of it during the past month has convinced me that it is not possible to get from them an amount of work approximate to the normal quantity which a man can perform while they are living under the exposure to the weather and to fire which at present obtains in the line of trenches which we hold. I consider that immediate steps should be taken to provide cover from the weather for the men and that their constructive work should be put aside until at least two thirds of the men are so provided. I am fully convinced that if this is done the result will be a quicker completion of the programme of work than would be possible if it is allowed to continue with the men exposed as they are at present. It would, of course, also very considerably increase their capacity for work if these shelters were made splinter-proof, as although casualties from the enemy's shell fire have been very infrequent, the necessity for taking greater precaution to prevent these is at present very trying for the men and still further reduces their power to perform constructive work. From reading the Intelligence Summaries which come to me daily and from observations of the enemy, I consider that they have been for some time busily engaged in providing proper shelter for their men in the whole of their front line

(sgd) Bernard C. Green
Lt. Col.
Commanding LONDON Scott/1/14

1st Brigade.

1st Division.

Transferred to 56th Division 7.2.16.

L/14th BATTALION LONDON REGIMENT (LONDON SCOTTISH)

JANUARY 1916.

56

1st Div
1st Bde
1/14 London Regt
Jan
Vol XVI

To 57 Brig. 7.2.16.

To 0

WAR DIARY
or
INTELLIGENCE SUMMARY
(Erase heading not required.)

London Scottish
1/14 County London BN

Instructions regarding War Diaries and Intelligence Summaries are contained in F. S. Regs., Part II. and the Staff Manual respectively. Title pages will be prepared in manuscript.

Hour, Date, Place	Summary of Events and Information	Remarks and references to Appendices
1st January 1916 NOEUX-LES-MINES	The Battalion moved into Brigade in the WEST part of Philosophe (PHILOSOPHE) (rave, and was billeted). Colonel C.E. Stewart, C.M.G., commanding 1st Black Watch on being appointed Brigadier General to another Brigade approached ... etc Commanding Officer his regret at having to be separated from the 1st Brigade and from the Battalion that had served so long beside him and he referred in very pleasant terms to the friendship that had grown up between his battalion and the London Scottish.	
2nd & 3rd January 1916 At PHILOSOPHE	In reserve	
4th Jan '16	Battalion relieved the 10th Gloucesters in the trenches, opposite hits at ÉLIE, introducing in about 800 yards SOUTH of the Road from VERMELLES to HULLUCH. On boundary of the Royal Scots Rifles being attacked for instruction. German	The 1st Cameron Highlanders being on our right flank, and the unit of a cavalry Division on our left.
7th Jan '16	Battalion moved back into support in old fields front line and back to the front line on the 10th. Relieved by the 11th Royal Scots (MAZINGARBE), 15th Div. Moved to ÉLIE in Mazingarbe (MAZINGARBE) Divisional reserve.	
Night of 13/14th		
14th Oct. 16th. BURBURE	Battalion moved by motor bus to Burbure and into billets there (BURBURE) S of LILLERS	

1247 W 3299 200,000 (E) 8/14 J.B.C. & A. Forms/C. 2118/11.

WAR DIARY
or
INTELLIGENCE SUMMARY
(Erase heading not required.)

LONDON SCOTTISH
1/14 County of LONDON REGT

Instructions regarding War Diaries and Intelligence Summaries are contained in F. S. Regs., Part II. and the Staff Manual respectively. Title pages will be prepared in manuscript.

Hour, Date, Place	Summary of Events and Information	Remarks and references to Appendices
20th January 1916. BURBURE	The following letter was received from 1st Div. "General Sir Henry Rawlinson, commanding 1st Army desires me to convey to the General Commanding and officers, non-commissioned officers and men of 14t Battalion, his appreciation of the work they have done in the reconstruction of the trenches between the 'HULLUCH ROAD and LOOS.' The Army Commander considers that they have landed them over a model of what trenches should be, and that this reflects very great credit on the 14t division as a whole. He wishes me to convey his congratulations to them on the point." The Battalion supplies a Guard of Honour of 3 officers and 10th O.Ranks on the occasion of General Gough's visit to the district. The following letter was received in connection with same. From 1st Div. to 1st Bat. "The Officer – General desires you to convey to the O.C. LONDON SCOTTISH his appreciation of the manner in which the Guard of Honour at LILLERS was turned out. The Soundin that the turn out, the handling of arms and steadiness on parade were quite exceptional, and was much gratified thereby.	

(signed) Malcolm Allan
Capt Off?

Army Form C. 2118.

Instructions regarding War Diaries and Intelligence
Summaries are contained in F. S. Regs., Part II.
and the Staff Manual respectively. Title pages
will be prepared in manuscript.

WAR DIARY

or

INTELLIGENCE SUMMARY

(Erase heading not required.)

LONDON SCOTTISH
1/14 City of London REGT.

Hour, Date, Place	Summary of Events and Information	Remarks and references to Appendices
20th January Contd. BURBURE	From 1st Batt. to C.O. LONDON SCOTTISH The Brigadier General fully endorses the above and sympathises with the trend of Honour over their disappointment at not being inspected by the French Commander-in-Chief, owing to change of plans, especially after the trouble all ranks took to live up to their reputation under adverse circumstances. *Honours & Awards* The following are extracts from LONDON GAZETTE d. 13/1/16. To be Honorary Major. Hon. Capt. W.E. WEBB 14 (Co. of London) Battn. LONDON REGT. T.F., with effect from Jany 1st '16 inclusive. Capt. H.C. Syer has been awarded the Military Cross for valuable service rendered in connection with the war. The following Officers and N.C.O have been mentioned in despatches. Capt. C.G.J Low, D.S.O. 2/ Capt. A.B. Syer 2/ Capt. W.L. Chaplin (Died of Wounds) 2/ Lieut J.E. Steele Hon. Capt. & QM. W.E. WEBB	

Capt H.H.L.

WAR DIARY

OR

INTELLIGENCE SUMMARY

(Erase heading not required.)

Instructions regarding War Diaries and Intelligence Summaries are contained in F. S. Regs., Part II. and the Staff Manual respectively. Title pages will be prepared in manuscript.

LONDON SCOTTISH
1/14 Bttn of LONDON REGT

Hour, Date, Place	Summary of Events and Information	Remarks and references to Appendices
20th January. BURBURE	Honours + Awards (contd) The late Lieut. G. L. Grant R.A.M.C. Rev. R. A. Stewart (Chaplain) No. 1311 Sgt. R. McLagan The following are extracts from LONDON GAZETTE d. 13/1/16. To be companion of the Distinguished Service Order Lt (Temp. Capt) H. H. H. Wewington Awarded the Military Cross 2nd Lieut (Tp Capt) S. Lyall Grant 2nd Lieut (Tp. Lieut) J. E. Knee Awarded the Distinguished Conduct Medal No. 178 (now 2nd/Lieut) W. Anderson " 192th (now 2nd/Lieut) G. F. Burn " 484 L.Q.M.S (now Q.M) Clb Fraser " 14 Clb Sh. (now Tp Lt) Wm. Kirby Battalion in training at BURBURE	
21st–31st January '16		

1247   W 8299 200,000 (E) 8/14 J.B.C. & A.   Forms/C. 2118/11.

Cupt 1/14